A BUSINESS PLANNER
FOR THE
BUSINESS STARTER

DR STÉPHANE-LAURE CAUBET

Copyright © 2020 Dr Stéphane-Laure Caubet.

All rights reserved. No part of this book may be reproduced, stored, or transmitted by any means—whether auditory, graphic, mechanical, or electronic—without written permission of the author, except in the case of brief excerpts used in critical articles and reviews. Unauthorized reproduction of any part of this work is illegal and is punishable by law.

ISBN: 978-1-7169-3529-9 (sc)
ISBN: 978-1-7164-8410-0 (e)

Library of Congress Control Number: 2020917932

Because of the dynamic nature of the Internet, any web addresses or links contained in this book may have changed since publication and may no longer be valid. The views expressed in this work are solely those of the author and do not necessarily reflect the views of the publisher, and the publisher hereby disclaims any responsibility for them.

Any people depicted in stock imagery provided by Getty Images are models,
and such images are being used for illustrative purposes only.
Certain stock imagery © Getty Images.

Lulu Publishing Services rev. date: 10/12/2020

To Arnaud and Zoé.

Thanks to Isabelle, Kannan, Caroline, and Camille.

CONTENTS

How to Use This Guide... xi
Preface xiii
Entrepreneurship is a New Global Trend.......................................xvii
Introduction... xxv
    Why the Business Plan Matters...xxvi
    What Is a Business Plan, and Why Do We Need One? xxvii
    What Do the Entrepreneurs Who Succeed Have? xxxiii

Chapter 1: Search for the Idea: Ideation 1
    The Nature of Ideas... 7
        Case Study: Is the idea the most important
        part of a business? 7
    Five Tips to Turn Your Idea into a Business 10
        Ideation Exercises 12
        Freewriting exercise 15
        Why Leadership Matters 17

Chapter 2: Summarize the Activity 19

Chapter 3: Show the Potential of the Market 29
    Who Are My Customers?... 33
    The Competitors 35
    Be a Strategist 41
        What is this analysis for? 51

Understanding the Environment of the Sector
(STEEPLE Analysis) 53
    The use 53
Understanding Your Environment (SWOT Analysis).................... 55
    The use 55
    With SMART Goals 56
Case Study: Tennis School SWOT Example 58

Chapter 4: Structure Your Business 61
What if the Market Doesn't Exist? 65
The Value Proposition 66
The Business Model 69
How to Summarize the Hypothesis 70
The Business Model Canvas 70
Case Study: Start with the non-scalable 71

Chapter 5: Select Your Legal Form 73
Secure your development: Minimize the risk or calculate it 74
Legal System Overview 75
Investment 77
Incorporating 77
Employment 78
Intellectual Property 78

Chapter 6: Suggest a Financial Plan 83
Start-Up Costs 85
Income Statement 86
Balance Sheet Example 87
Projected Cash Flow Example 88
Are Investors in it just for money? 89
How to Pitch 95
Some Common and Practical Tips... 97
Five Tips to Convince Others in Two Minutes 98

Chapter 7: Set Up Your Business Plan 99
    Business Plan Outline 101

Chapter 8: Start Your Business 105
    Why Do People Become Entrepreneurs? 106
    Uncertainty in Entrepreneurship... 107
    Entrepreneur Portrait 110
        Arnaud 110

Conclusion 113
Bibliography..115
Online Sources..117

HOW TO USE THIS GUIDE

This guide is geared towards entrepreneurs. The information and suggestions herein are based on my personal experience and on that of my clients.

In the 2010s, I, like most people, was shocked by the news that 80 percent of companies fail within the first five years of coming into existence. I wondered at that time what a difference it would make if these enterprises had both relevant information and support. Would it affect their survival rate?[1]

Interestingly, studies show that after the first five years of operation, 70 percent of companies that have been accompanied are still running and have become viable. This marks a real difference. Whatever solution an entrepreneur finds when starting a company will be beneficial for the business's survival at this critical moment in its life.

This guide outlines the method 8S2Business uses with the early-stage entrepreneur. It is an informative management tool to help the entrepreneur realize his or her idea and implement his or her plan.

---

[1] "Survie des entreprises à 5 ans," Petite-Enterprise, November 19, 2012, https://www.petite-entreprise.net/P-137-87-G1-survie-des-entreprises-a-5-ans.html; Marion Bain, "77% des auto-entreprises meurent avant cinq ans," L'Express, September 19, 2017, https://lentreprise.lexpress.fr/creation-entreprise/auto-entrepreneur/77-des-auto-entrepreneurs-periclitent-avant-cinq-ans_1944901.html.

PREFACE

Having a job doing something that was clearly not what I wanted to be doing helped me to understand that I should perhaps concentrate my efforts on what I loved to do instead.

At the end of my studies, I entered the corporate world and was happy to be independent, but I missed the fun, and I was unable to find true satisfaction with my work. I was focused on finding happiness in my personal life and felt it was acceptable to have a professional life and a job that was adequate to afford me a decent income. At some point, I was fortunate to join a company where I was able to combine fun, friends, and money. Once I discovered that such a thing existed, I changed my focus to finding fulfillment in my job, preferably within my area of expertise.

I always wanted to be happy, like most people, and like most people I had focused on having a good job, a great car, and a nice apartment.

When I finally had acquired all these things, I did not feel happy. It's not that I was sad or unhappy, just unfulfilled. I had a "*So what?*" state of mind, often experiencing the kind of moment where you wonder, "*Is that all there is? Will my life be like this forever?*"

I did not feel comfortable with having such thoughts. I was ashamed since really, I considered myself lucky to have achieved all those things in my twenties. I started looking for something else: my purpose.

I did not have the name for it at the time, but I began talking more and more about something that would give meaning to my life. I wanted to be useful.

My own experience and that of the people whom I met over the years led me to realize that most of the time we place ourselves in situations that make us uncomfortable, circumstances that we choose to accept. "Don't let others define who you are" is something that I have learned the meaning of the hard way.

Meeting amazing people with inspiring life journeys opened my eyes. They seemed weird, crazy, utopian, or out of their minds because they had chosen to be or to do something unexpected or different.

I was fortunate to meet a woman who decided to change her life at the age of fifty by changing careers, going from being a doctor to becoming a life coach. I met two other such people on the same day: a twenty-three-year-old woman who had chosen not to take a super job in London so she could open her own company in Vietnam instead and a future lawyer who had chosen to be an activist in her country and build an NGO.

I came across a millionaire who wished to do better than his father in managing the family business. After taking a trip around the world, he decided to be a life coach.

All these people are entrepreneurs. They each have a story to tell that shows their will to try to do the thing or to build the thing that they are meant to do or to build.

They sacrifice many things that others would not easily let go of, such as money, family and friends. Entrepreneurs are, in my opinion, people who face their fears and their doubts in order to overcome them. I have learned from my clients that managing uncertainty requires the humility and courage to face your own vulnerability and to overcome self-doubt[2]. I

---

[2] Brenée Brown. "The power of vulnerability: Teaching of Authenticity, Connections and courage" published April 2013

now understand why we admire people who do things that others would not do. These people inspire us because they face seemingly impossible situations and yet get through them.

Through reading many books and watching even more videos, I have discovered and learned many things such as this TED talk given by Emily Esfahani Smith, who is very simple and efficient in her approach to highlighting the difference between being happy and having meaning in life. She claims that this meaning comes from serving something greater than yourself, whereas happiness comes and goes.

In her talk, Emily Esfahani Smith presented the four pillars of meaning, as seen in the following image:

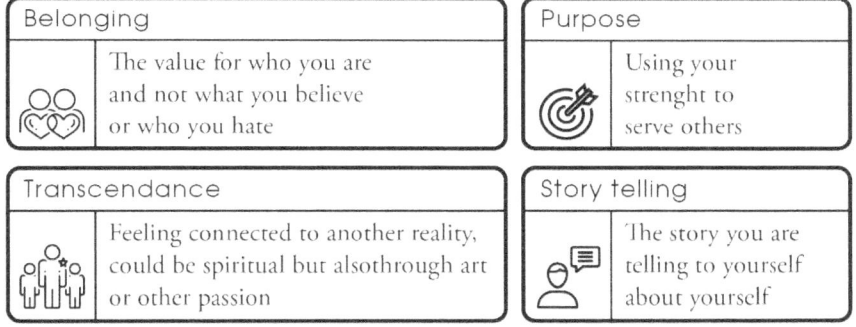

Belonging, purpose, transcendence, and storytelling

At some point after I'd met all sorts of people who were building something, working on a project, or starting up a company and sharing with others who they were and what they were doing with their lives, I was led to literally face my own search for meaning.

I later realized that I needed to share what this search for meaning is about with other people. I believe that this is how it became my purpose to help others.

ENTREPRENEURSHIP IS A NEW GLOBAL TREND

Each new generation arrives with the dream of disrupting the market. New work tools are born from new technologies.

Today, many young entrepreneurs wish to change the institutional and organizational working environment and the whole labor market. People are tired of working just to make a living. There is a growing number of people who wish to mix their work with their hobbies to live out their passions. It's not very common to see someone build a career in a specific field and one day completely change their path to focus on something that they are truly passionate about, something that makes them happy enough that they find it easy to get up in the morning and go to work.

Nowadays, new workers are in search of personal growth more than merely seeking a paycheck. And guess what? They aren't alone!

Studies show that millennials believe businesses should be more ethical and society-focused, but they remain wary of the motives of certain companies. Sixty-four percent believe that businesses focus more on their own agenda than on considering the wider society. 58 percent believe that businesses behave ethically. 57 percent agree that business leaders are committed to helping to improve society, and 54 percent agree that many businesses have no ambition beyond wanting to make money.

We can see that in most of these situations, the new generation of workers behave differently and expect something more than just a job.

Based on the foregoing observations, we can conclude that new workers believe that the motives of certain companies do not fully meet their expectations as employees. This gives us an indication of how these new workers might feel at work.

More and more workers are looking for a career change.[3] Studies have shown that many people feel miserable at work.[4]

In the UK, a study indicates that of the people between the ages of eighteen and twenty-four, 68 percent feel miserable at work, and of the people between twenty-five and thirty-four years old, 65 percent feel miserable. Interestingly the percentage continues on its downward trend for the group between the ages of thirty-five and forty-four, with 52 percent of them sharing the same feeling of being very unhappy at work.

The number dips below 50 percent for people forty-five to fifty-four years old, 43 percent of whom feel miserable at work, and for those fifty-five years of age or older, 19 percent feel miserable at work.

Times are changing. No longer do workers blindly respect the authority of those in charge. The previous generation respected their managers even if they did not agree with the strategies in place. They wanted to do their jobs, be promoted, and so on.

Now people still want to succeed, but the definition of success is changing. No longer are managers the ones who decided what is most important to focus on at work. The younger workers ask questions and want an answer fast so that they may act on it.

---

[3] Peter Fleming, "The Trials of a 2016 Job: Why So Many of Us Are Unhappy at Work," *The Guardian*, May 9, 2016, https://www.theguardian.com/commentisfree/2016/may/09/trails-of-2016-job-low-satisfaction-company-short-termism.

[4] Rebecca Burn Callander, "It's Official: Most People Are Miserable at Work," the *Telegraph*, September 18, 2015, http://www.telegraph.co.uk/finance/jobs/11871751/Its-official-most-people-are-miserable-at-work.html.

Nowadays, we can use the internet to learn to do most things. Thanks to the wide selection of educational and informational videos available, people do not feel that they need a more experienced person to learn from. Now they can learn most anything and do it faster than previously imaginable.

I remember participating in a conference on start-ups with a panel of four experienced people (an architect, an entrepreneur, an adviser, and an investor) presenting their experience with entrepreneurship. One young guy raised his hand at the Q and A session and shared his point. He explained that for him, schools and universities were no longer useful. He said that nowadays we do not need degrees to make things, because we can find everything on the internet. He believed that degrees were meaningless and a waste of time. Most people in the audience clapped their hands and nodded their heads in approval and affirmation.

To be honest, I was struggling with this idea. I agree that schools and universities should adapt and change their programs to make learning more practical. But like one of the panelists answered, if you need to get brain surgery, you want your surgeon to have completed medical school instead of having spent his or her time watching videos to learn how to perform brain surgery.

With the accessibility of knowledge, authority is no longer justified by a person's position. How workers feel about their managers or bosses is often based on their reputation and management style.

It is becoming common for an employee to evaluate and give marks to the manager, for the students to evaluate the teacher, and for the clients to give stars on a mobile application to its driver.

So, what matters for workers today?

In most markets, work-life balance comes before career progression when workers are evaluating their job opportunities. Studies show the relative degree of importance of a good work-life balance. Next in importance is the opportunity to progress and eventually become a leader. In the third position is flexibility (whether working remotely or having leadership opportunities), which appears to be a major factor in terms of quality of work.

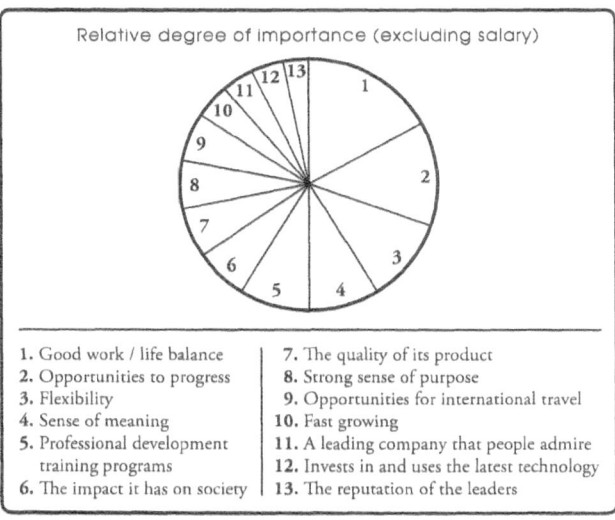

Relative degree of importance

Most of the time frustration leads us to stay in a job we do not like, do work that we do not care about at a company that we do not even believe in. How can we expect ourselves or our colleagues, bosses, and employees to excel in everything we and they do? It is true that we will excel at what we enjoy and perform less competently in what we do not enjoy. It is only human!

How then are companies supposed to capture our interest? Obviously, by allowing us to do what we love to do so we do it better, and not by having us do simply what they want us to do.

Historically, employers have offered entry-level positions on a "take it or leave it" basis. The underlying belief is that everyone must pay their dues. It was even worse for the generation before as this was the mindset of people filling most positions. The economic situation was different, leading people to accept and tolerate being treated badly.[5]

---

[5] Brett Cenkus, "Millennials Will Work Hard, Just Not for Your Crappy Job," the Start-Up, November 16, 2017, https://medium.com/swlh/millennials-will-work-hard-just-not-for-your-crappy-job-82c12a1853ed.

From the beginning, this new generation has refused to place themselves in the types of situations that the previous generation accepted, with long hours and low recognition or consideration, especially at the entry level.[6]

Despite a growing desire for a better work-life balance, according to a 2016 survey by the American Psychological Association, only 53 percent of workers say that their employers value work-life balance, and only 43 percent say that their employers offer programs and policies that allow for flexibility.[7]

When we asked younger millennials (graduates and holders of junior positions) what factors were "very influential" in their decision-making process at work, they responded as follows:

- their personal values/morals
- their personal goals and ambitions with regard to career progression
- the impact that they would make on clients and customers
- holding true to the organization's values or overall sense of purpose
- meeting the organization's values or objectives (profit and targets)
- avoiding trouble and minimizing personal risk
- the impact that they would make on colleagues

It is important to shine a light upon our way of thinking about work and to discern why the current direction and trend suggests a move toward entrepreneurship.

It is the purpose of this guide to provide information that can help you and provide you with analytical tools so that you may gain a better understanding of entrepreneurship, which may inspire you to reflect more deeply on your own time.

---

[6] Jeffery G. Harber, "Generations in the Workplace: Similarities and Differences" (PhD diss., East Tennessee State University, 2011).
[7] Ryan Jenkins, "This Is Why Millennials Care So Much about Work-Life Balance," *Inc.* magazine, January 8, 2018, https://www.inc.com/ryan-jenkins/this-is-what-millennials-value-most-in-a-job-why.html.

Indeed, beyond the economic reasons arising from the current context, the change in the labor market is also attributable to the new generation of workers.

If we take a look at the ideas about the current generation that are circulating, we find a trend emerging. Generation X and Generation Y are, for the most part, made up of active people.

If we follow sociological data to give us a basis for reflection, the data on these generations only reinforces the current trend.

Emerging in 1993, coined by *Advertising Age* magazine, the term *Generation Y* indicates the generation after Generation X. Americans also use the term *digital natives* to point to the fact that these people were born into using a computer. Sometimes the terms are shortened to "Gen X" or "Gen Y" with individuals referred to as Gen X'ers and Gen Y'ers.

This generation is, in my opinion, a generation of innovative people. They innovate to help society withstand crisis situations such as war; to improve social standing; and to navigate through pandemics such as AIDS for example, which this generation has always known. In addition to innovating, they also embody a collaborative spirit.

Indeed, we are beginning to see more and more talented people who do not have what are seen to be good qualifications or a good profile in the conventional sense. If we think about the things that we have traditionally considered, then we will miss discovering the talent that lies among the new generation of workers.

When we open our minds to this concept, we can easily picture an outgoing business school student deciding to become a tennis teacher. A dentist may decide to become a personal development coach. A lawyer specializing in business law may decide, instead of practicing law, to become a director of human resources or perhaps directing a real estate agency.

Generation Y will make up 75 percent of the workforce in 2025. At that point, they will be the ones to define culture and business expectations.[8]

Some people learn early on what professional field suits them best, but for others who aren't so quick to find out what type of work they would like to do, the evolution of modern society, even more than before, allows them to embark on a non-traditional career path.

These are the people who rethink the trades and our ways of working. Anyone with access to knowledge can specialize in the field of their choice.

The focus is no longer on knowledge but on what a person is able to do with it.

Beyond the business itself, there is the human factor, which is present in any business.

Keep in mind that co-operative communities which help and support each other are on the rise. These start-up communities exist everywhere from Vietnam to California. They are characterized by forums, "coworking" spaces and events focusing on a variety of topics that are of great interest to these communities. In other words, we are seeing a gathering of entrepreneurs sharing the same purpose and the same mindset.

At the same time, community programs are expanding to teach entrepreneurs how to turn their big ideas into innovative start-ups. Organizations are hosting networking events and providing training programs, assistance programs, start-up acceleration programs, work materials, and expertise. The point is to ensure that entrepreneurs get the guidance that they need to structure their projects and present them effectively.

We see big companies organizing events like business plan competitions or creating in-house incubators to seek creativity, youthful thinking, and innovative solutions to apply to their businesses.

---

[8] BNP Paribas, "Global Entrepreneur Report 2016: 3 HC Coaching."

Entrepreneurship is gaining value in society.

Is it entrepreneurship or the mindset of entrepreneurship that is the new trend?

Anybody can have an idea, but not everybody can make it a business and then lead that business as an entrepreneur?

INTRODUCTION

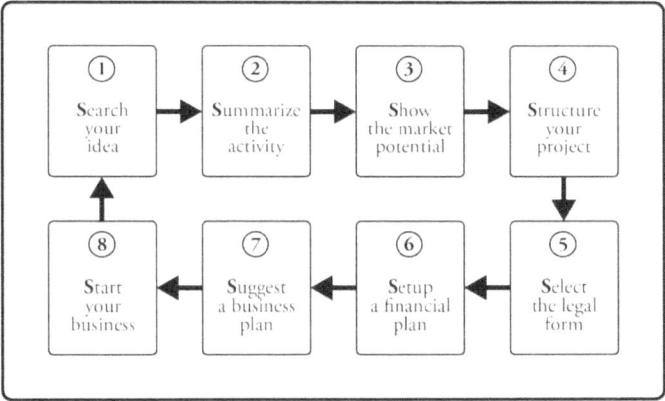

The 8S method

In a broader sense, I see the logic of the 8S method as it may apply to all the business projects of a given company. The steps are inspired directly by the business plan structure.

The number 8 allows for some cutting of the steps, leading to the end point of each step. But first a company must take it step by step so as not to miss out on any important issues in the implementation of the project. The number itself is of less importance than the steps we focus on in this process and on their progress and implementation.

The object is to logically order the steps needed to achieve a result. It is therefore essential to understand that in taking these steps, you are laying the foundation to build and develop the project and to ask the right questions to give life to the project.

The question is not the number of steps you follow to structure your project but what you need to do to make it real. I am not proposing something rigid; the method should be understood as a set of guidelines that will help you to find, and then to follow, your path. Each of us has our own 8S. Even if there are some common needs, each case will present its own unique needs.

Why the Business Plan Matters

First of all, the business plan is a communication tool that will allow you to present the value of your project. Its purpose is to be convincing. It allows the entrepreneur to convince others to buy or sell his product or service or to contribute to his project.

In reality, people seem to avoid implementing a business plan, especially at the start, because at that point the business is not yet stable. At the start-up of a business, no one knows what is going to happen, so they make projections and propose hypotheses.

Some entrepreneurs may do some business planning with the plan working more or less as expected, but others might allow an image of the business to arise so as to realize the initial idea. At the beginning, the first draft of your ideation process will change, needing to be reorganized later, but it is a starting point.

Some authors, entrepreneurs, and professionals tend to think that because business planning is not an exact science, the business plan is useless. I don't think that this is the case. I think that this uncertainty is inherent in the exercise. It is also part of the job of the entrepreneur who needs to be able to deal with both opportunities and an unstable situation.

It is true that the business plan changes all the time; it is part of the uncertainty of entrepreneurship. The entrepreneur needs to be able to manage a difficult and unpredictable situation. Indeed, an entrepreneur cannot grow his or her business or develop his or her idea without facing challenges. The thing is that by definition, the challenges would be considered something else if they were comfortable things to deal with. As many other authors have mentioned, you need to get out of your comfort zone to be able to manage your business.

What Is a Business Plan, and Why Do We Need One?

When you are an entrepreneur, you have an idea; you want to do something, and what you are proposing is new. Then you do research on the internet to find advice and videos on topics such as the following:

- the five mistakes you should avoid
- the ten points for writing an efficient business plan
- whether or not you should hire a consultant
- whether or not you should use a specific type of software

You may also look into testimonials about the following things:

- how to launch a company
- how to create a company without spending money

In the end, there is a lot of information coming from many sources, and despite our best intentions to try and learn from others, at some point we get lost. This is the reason why I insisted earlier on the importance of building your business and on taking certain steps according to the path that you're on.

It won't be easy to build your business, but difficulty is part of the game. Your commitment is necessary to reach your goal.

As Mahatma Gandhi said, "Satisfaction lies in the effort, not in the attainment. Full effort is full victory." Writing a business plan is not fancy, but it is part of the job.

When you start your company, you need to be ready to experience both ups and downs, as we know the road is not smooth but full of bumps. Having a map helps us to be sure that we are continuing to move forward and to make the best decisions that we can make based on our goals and on our will power.

At my company we are used to working with incubators for companies that have yet to get off the ground to help them grow and get to the next level. We have even helped schools whose main method was to focus on the following points:

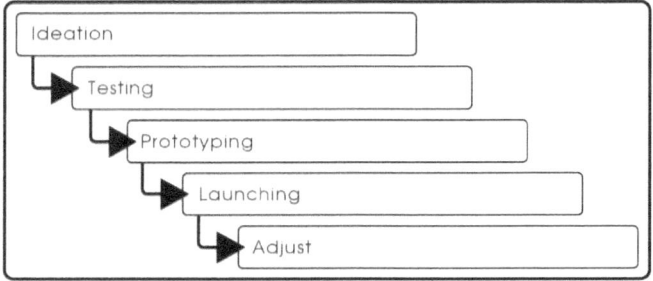

The process, from the idea to its implementation

This process is quite popular particularly in the IT industry. The method itself is not an issue. We understand the concept well. My question is, "when will you start making money?" I find the structure efficient and relevant. However, it represents only a third of our method.

We used to observe it often when hearing business pitch presentations, particularly the financial projections. A good business plan makes the difference between presenting a project and presenting a plausible business.

We often see businesses that arise out of an entrepreneur's hobby. This is totally fine. In many cases what the person is already doing can be transformed into a business, albeit in some other form. However, depending on the time, energy, and money available, an entrepreneur may not progress beyond the stage of wishing to start the business.

This, however, does not explain or justify every business failure. I mention it only to point out something we often see when companies are pitching to raise capital. Despite a great idea and a viable project, the focus is more on the technological aspects and less on the business, the latter of which is the language investors will understand. It helps them to plan their investment in the business.

I will share here the program of an incubator that has been operating for more than ten years in Europe and propose a start-up incubation program.

This famous incubator uses a three-month method to get businesses off the ground using a program that is divided into two parts:

- ⇨ Problem solving and creativity
- ⇨ Prototyping and business strategy

What happens after the three-month program? The company solves a problem, prototypes its product and finds a business strategy.

When the entrepreneurs are alone, they then face the reality of running and building a business and at this point it leaves the "lab" and enters the real world.

This is the moment when the entrepreneur needs to start looking for clients, gain traction and prove that the business is able to generate revenue and grow.

We noticed that a few entrepreneurs seemed a bit lost after the incubation program. They were facing the market and trying to continue to develop their projects. A few of them gave up, but for those who continued, the challenge remained.

There is for every entrepreneur that we have met (and we have met a few, ourselves included) this lonely moment when he is alone facing his business idea with each day a blank page on which to write his story.

At that point, the entrepreneur needs courage and nerves of steel to decide to carry on with all of the work that needs to be done. Each day they do the best that they can to move forward step by step.

I do not want to sound dramatic here, but I used to tell my business associates how it was when I started my company and registered my domain name. At that point, I had a professional email address, a website under construction, and nothing else. I received no emails. No one knew me or what I was doing. I was alone with my blank page, and I knew that I needed to go out and present my work and my ideas to people, face their judgment, or get their interest.

As an entrepreneur, it is often a requirement to face your fears while screening out other people's fears and their grim projections for your business. I consider this to be a place of freedom, but it can be scary.

On the other hand, we've also seen that doing nothing can eat up a person's energy. Therefore, at least try to realize your dream, instead of being a prisoner of other's people's fears.

Whom Do You Admire?

This small question is one of the more interesting ones I used to ask my clients. It is also one that I ask myself a lot.

Whom do you admire? Just looking for the answer to this question brings some positivity. It is quite an amazing feeling. I love asking this question whenever my client, my team, or I feel a little bit down.

It is interesting because this idea brings both hope and inspiration. You do not want to give up like someone you barely respect. You want to fight for something that inspires you like the extraordinary person whom you admire.

We admire extraordinary people, the ones who do not follow a straight line but who do something different from what other people are doing.

The doubt, the fear of failure, and the fear of being judged may all block the growth process and the development of an idea. However, if the idea is a compelling one, it raises your level of conviction.

Most of the time, we admire someone because of something she has done or is doing and that you would love to be able to do. It might be raising a child, building something large or small, trying to do something new, fighting for an important cause, or believing in something when no one else does.

It helps to see that despite the doubt and the uncertainty of the result, things are indeed possible.

Knowing this does not mean that the doubt disappears, but in the balance, it becomes (depending on the situation) less present or seems less important.

This positively allows projection, looking ahead to reach a goal instead of looking down, afraid of every step you are taking.

List three persons you admire, describe them, and explain why you admire them:

What Do the Entrepreneurs Who Succeed Have?

To finalize a business project, four essential elements are required: the idea, the money, time, and the drive.

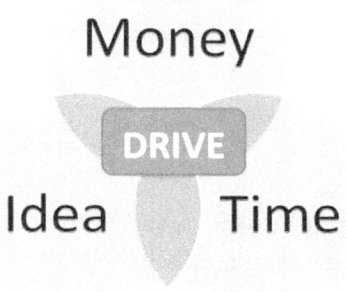

Idea, money, time, drive

The more I work and the more I discover other entrepreneurs from all over the world (Vietnam, Singapore, France, Italy, Poland, America, Australia, et al.), the more I see common ground.

An entrepreneur is not some kind of crazy person willing to go on come what may. Neither is she or he looking for a way to become rich as soon as possible, for the most part. However, the ones who succeed in the serious work of building a company are the ones who do not quit. Getting little sleep, they work hard and dare to do the things.

Entrepreneurs dare to dream about themselves, about their project, and about their vision. They become what they do.

Even though we know of and admire many famous entrepreneurs, the evidence of whose success is all around us, we tend to ignore the many other entrepreneurs around us who dare to strike out on their own. Our first reaction most of the time when an entrepreneur mentions his or her idea is often to laugh, thinking, "Are you sure?" We give them no more than three years before they fail. At a later stage, we ask, "Did you make money with your product?" And then if the person starts earning a living from his or her business, we ask no more questions, seeing the evidence. Then what was once the entrepreneur's innovative dream becomes an everyday thing.

Getting back to the entrepreneurs who succeed, it is important to know that the definition of success is subjective. When I talk about success, I am talking more about accomplishment than the amount of money in a person's bank account. Not all entrepreneurs are celebrities, but they are able to earn a living from the businesses that they have developed.

This is what success is when you succeed in developing your product and making it work. This part is less fancy than the entrepreneur success stories we are used to reading or hearing about, but these types of entrepreneurs are independent and more numerous.

To be honest, it is a good thing to have the drive to start up a business, but many other things need to be implemented before you reach your goal.

There is no business without the client. People need to be interested in your product and ready to buy it if your company is to remain in business.

Based on my experience, without the four elements of idea, money, time, and drive, an entrepreneur has a lower chance of successfully completing the project of building a business around a product.

The best lesson about entrepreneurship that I have learned is that one must have the ability to overcome hardships that may seem insurmountable.

I have met people who made the impossible possible by the sheer force of their ideas, which are visions, and the strength of their convictions, which allows them to take on a big project and build a business.

The four elements of idea, money, time and drive are interdependent. What's more, these elements are nothing without the person behind them. That's why I put drive in the center of the diagram, as the drive cannot exist without a person's intention.

I strongly believe that despite automation, humans have a crucial place in our society. Despite the growing role of new technologies, it is human vision and human strength that allows us to transform and evolve. It is part of the essence of our society.

This is the reason why I see entrepreneurship as a particularly important element to highlight a vision to help improve our daily lives.

Entrepreneurs have extraordinary ideas for changing our lives. Without the vision, the will, the perseverance, and the courage of humans, we would still think that the earth is flat and that it is impossible for a person to walk on the moon.

I choose to help people starting a business because I see the path that they are traveling on and what they have to accomplish before they can see their dreams come true. This is where my *drive* comes from to do everything possible to help make the impossible possible.

Returning to our discussion about the four elements, it is necessary to have money in order to set up a business. I won't lie, without money, it becomes much more complicated. Ask yourself the following question: *If I have a lot of money, can I start a successful business?*

It is probably easier to start a business and plan to hire very competent people, but this is not necessarily a guarantee of success, because without a solid idea, the path also becomes complicated!

Note that these four elements are not easy to put in place at the very beginning. You may be able to gather several of them, but to have a good handle on them all when you are starting a project is rare.

Entrepreneurs often have one (or more) of the following combinations:

- time and money, but no idea or drive
- time, the idea, and the drive, but no money
- the drive, the idea, and the money, but not the time (or some other factor).

Not having all the best cards in your hand is not the greatest concern. Whereas it may be worrying and stressful, it is not insurmountable. It's even part of the game.

As in life, it is not always those who do not have the best game who lose the game. The criteria of time, money, and idea are external elements that can be acquired. Indeed, to find money, it is possible to borrow. To find the time, you can take it. To find an idea, you can buy a company or take on a partner with the right talents and skills.

But this is where the drive comes in. The drive is the element that makes the project possible. It makes the difference between bringing the project to life and letting it die.

I have been fortunate in recent years to meet entrepreneurs from different backgrounds, all of them offering different things but still finding themselves facing similar difficulties.

I like to quote Oscar Wilde's saying, "Experience is the name everyone gives to their mistakes." This aphorism summarizes in one sentence what we live daily as entrepreneurs.

The insight comes when we realize that mistakes are part of the plan. The greater our ability to cope positively with failure, the more humility, courage, perseverance, and resilience we will exhibit.

Rather than seeing things as a failure, most entrepreneurs see them as experiences and as feedback that can even become opportunities.

It is these errors that lead to a good result. Without making mistakes, we do not move forward.

CHAPTER 1

SEARCH FOR THE IDEA: IDEATION

> Knowing is not enough; we must apply.
> Willing is not enough; we must do.

Johann Wolfgang von Goethe, German writer and statesman, 1749–1832

In order to succeed, we need more than an idea. What is needed is a vision—a vision that can drive a project and take it to the next level.

To realize a project, we need commitment and leadership. We will come back to these two points later.

The first step to achieving success is to get an idea. This is the starting point. It may sound simple, but when we think about it for a minute, we quickly realize that it is not so obvious.

You may have more than one idea. The question then is "which one could be feasible?" Your idea may relate to a passion, to expertise, or to innovation itself, but is it viable?

The idea alone is nothing. You must study and analyze it to create a structure. A successful project is based not only on the idea but also on its application and implementation.

Thus, according to the 8S method, the idea is only one-eighth of what is required to build a company. One idea does not lead to the realization of a business or a project. It is the structure of the project that allows us to succeed in creating the product and starting a business.

To shape the idea and allow it to emerge, a set of attributes is necessary.

After finding an idea that seems workable and that corresponds to what you want to do, it is necessary to delimit it, define it, and analyze it.

You must understand the idea and shape it according to your vision. During the ideation phase of your business plan, you must determine whether you have an idea with which you could eventually generate business.

The goal, therefore, is not to have many ideas, but to have one good idea. But before finding this one good idea, you often encounter several pitfalls.

There are several types of entrepreneurs. We will consider two examples to illustrate the different issues these entrepreneurs may encounter.

Some entrepreneurs wish to change jobs because they do not thrive in their current jobs for various reasons. Instead, they have a passion and a skill that is not necessarily related to their trade. They wonder if they could live out their passion. When we talk about passion, we are referring to things such as photography, golf, cooking, travel, knitting, and gardening for example.

What is interesting here is that we already have an idea and, even more important, a passion. Passion makes a difference when you are presenting and defending the product or the project. With passion, you bring more than just your expertise. You bring a part of yourself from deep inside.

It is easy for people convince their audiences of the merits of their stories if they have "stars in their eyes" and infect them with their passion, enthusiasm and in some cases…charisma.

With this type of entrepreneur, the toughest part is not coming up with the idea itself but rather materializing it. Such an entrepreneur often has a more romantic, rather than pragmatic, approach to the project.

This is where the challenge lies. How does one monetize a passion and not just share it?

> **How does one monetize a passion and not just share it?**

Other entrepreneurs feel limited by the system within which they operate. They are part of the growing number of people who cannot imagine spending their entire careers at a single company or even living in just one country.

Members of the new generation are rethinking and rebuilding the economic system that has been in place for far too long. They have reached a point beyond which they cannot progress. Their job may be considered inadequate based on societal criteria such as degrees and professional qualifications. It is difficult for these people to break away from their areas of expertise. The ideas of this group of entrepreneurs tend to be more pragmatic than romantic.

The business advantage for them is that they give the people who follow or support them confidence.

How can I find an idea?

There is the traditional method of filling blank notebooks with ideas and hypotheses, since generally you may have more than one idea.

Take some time and answer the following questions:

What ideas have you had?

Think of ideas and inspirations that you have had, from a new product to a fleeting fancy.

_____
_____
_____
_____
_____
_____
_____
_____
_____
_____
_____
_____
_____
_____
_____

What about your skills?

_____
_____
_____

What activities do you enjoy doing?

What are your passions?

What did you want to do when you were a kid?

_____
_____
_____
_____
_____
_____
_____
_____
_____
_____
_____
_____

What type of issues do your relatives ask you for help with?

_____
_____
_____
_____
_____
_____
_____
_____
_____
_____
_____
_____
_____

The Nature of Ideas

Ideas demand change. Even if your idea is wonderful and brilliant, it will force someone, somewhere, to change how they do something. And for many people change is not easy. Doing something out of the ordinary and dealing with the unknown can be a challenge. Some individuals fear change so much that they structure their lives to avoid it.

At some point, complacency is a choice; the choice of doing the same job that you do not like or of staying in the same apartment in the same city and accepting it even if you find it miserable. Change is not easy, but neither is living a life you do not like. This is the reason why I talk about the choice to change or not.

Since many people do not like change and fear it, the merits of your idea may be precisely what make it so difficult for others to accept. So, when your great idea comes into contact with a person who does not want to change, you and your idea are not in a good place. In these situations, always remember to focus on your choice and follow your path.

From any stage of the entrepreneurial journey, we come back to this very first stage: "I have an idea!" But the idea isn't everything; the value you place on the idea is much more important.

The question at this point is whether the idea is feasible. It may be a passion, an area of expertise, or an innovation, but is it viable in terms of business?

Case Study: Is the idea the most important part of a business?

An idea alone is nothing. An idea can be good, even excellent, but if it is not relevant, or if it is difficult to implement, then it will have little value in terms of business. On the other hand, an idea some may consider to be neither good nor innovative could be very powerful in terms of business if executed well.

One of my first clients heard that I was in the early stages of building a company to help entrepreneurs build their businesses. He wanted me to support him in his idea of building a mobile application.

W was a worldwide internet-based mobile shopping application. Its goal was to get people to consume differently.

Despite a desire to be inventive, unique, instructive, playful, simple, and attractive, the creator of W was missing one quality: profitability. The founder did not wish to focus much on this point, which he considered to be secondary to the quality of the product that he was proposing. So we started to work on the feasibility study to see how we could concretely build this application.

The entrepreneur's confidence in his idea did not seem to be afflicted by any problems other than his not knowing how to implement it, but as the feasibility study progressed, the entrepreneur realized the importance of raising funds. Indeed, we were in the situation where the founder had the idea and the time but no money. This initial phase pointed out the strength of his drive, but more importantly he realized that he needed the funds first.

Why? The founder thought he would raise funds easily because to him, his idea seemed like such an appealing proposal for customers around the world that it would lead them to change their consumer habits. The problem was that these consumers had no idea of the existence of his application. Here is the thing: consumers have no idea what they are missing if they do not have the knowledge of the product. As we don't know what we don't know, being able to be seen, known, understood, and appreciated is a critical part of a business's success.

You cannot miss something you do not know exists.

The founder and I were targeting people living abroad, people traveling, or people just curious to discover other cultures. The more we progressed on the study, the more the founder felt disconcerted, not by the validity of his idea but by what was necessary just to make the project a reality.

We began talking about several partners who had made good offers and what they could bring to the business. We discussed how to make his product available to customers, the logistics needed, and the costs involved. He admitted later that he understood at this point that he was scared by all of this and that this was the reason why I had heard little from him. He and I stayed in touch, but his idea did not go any farther.

I am not saying that the idea is useless here. What I am saying is that it is a seed you need to water and nurture. It is the first step of a long journey.

Having an idea is definitely a good start, but the way you implement it can make all the difference!

One idea does not lead to the realization of a business or project. It is the structure of the plan to realize it that enables the entrepreneur to achieve his or her goal.

Five Tips to Turn Your Idea into a Business

1. Structure your idea.

First of all, your project has to be organized and structured to flow sequentially. This makes it easy to convert into a presentation for others to understand. You have to prove that you are motivated and ready to make your idea a reality through a well-developed plan. Keep the following considerations in mind:

- What is it about?
- Why are you doing it?
- How do you plan to achieve it?
- What tools will you use?
- How many partners will you have?
- How will you finance it?
- How will you acquire the right audience?
- What are your objectives?

2. Find your target.

Next you have to identify your market by defining your target customers while considering geographic and demographic data. You have to understand your customers, evaluate the size of your market, and ask yourself why people would purchase your product or your service.

Other considerations to take into account would be as follows:

- Whom are you addressing with your project?
- Is it a B2B or B2C business?
- Have you adapted it to the needs of your target audience?
- What value do you plan to add to this specific market?
- How do you plan to market your product online and/or off-line?

3. Evaluate the sustainability of your project.

The most important point is to conduct research to ensure that your project is sustainable. It can be simple to build a project, but many good projects fall into the trap of failing to find long-term market success.

Always be aware of your competitors and propose a strategy that makes you different.

4. Join communities.

Great communities exist in every city. You may choose to be connected online via forums or to meet up via networking events. Communities are there to offer support and to help with questions about building a project you that you may be considering.

Taking advantage of start-up communities is an interesting strategy because the members of these communities share the same mindset and can advise you to avoid the mistakes that they might have made before. You can brainstorm ideas and find solutions together to move forward.

5. Get assistance.

Remember, you are not alone. Train yourself and present your project to your family, friends, and acquaintances. Receiving feedback is essential for your development and for correcting weaknesses in the project.

At every stage, you also can contact a professional to assist you with every step of your business in order to save time.

Note: Spend money on services that allow you to avoid doing things you do not like doing.

Ideation Exercises

How would you see yourself if you were to realize your project?

Imagine yourself like in a 3D video game. Once you put on the virtual reality helmet, what do you see? Describe as much as you are able.

Where would you be?

_____
_____
_____
_____
_____
_____
_____
_____
_____
_____

In which kind of place would you live? Describe it or draw it.

_____
_____
_____
_____
_____
_____
_____
_____

In which country or city would you be?

What would your life be like?

How would the place where you work look? Describe it or draw it.

What would the place where you work look like? Describe it or draw it.

What would your typical day be like? What would you do?

Freewriting exercise

Freewriting is an ideation technique often used by writers. For creative people, it can help to *focus on the first stages of a new project* by establishing what you currently know and getting your initial ideas out of your head and onto paper.

Taking your central theme or topic, write down everything you currently know about the subject.

_____
_____
_____
_____
_____
_____
_____
_____
_____
_____

What do you need or want to know about the subject that you don't currently know? (Write down all the questions you have in mind regarding the topic.)

_____
_____
_____
_____
_____
_____
_____
_____
_____
_____

Why is this topic important?

___

What else do you have in mind?

___

This exercise is all about getting everything you can think of relating to your topic down on paper, *so don't be concerned if it looks messy.* The goal is just to get past the initial block.

Why Leadership Matters

Leadership is part of the process. Some entrepreneurs may have leadership skills from the beginning bolstered by strong self-esteem and self-confidence, while others need to learn how to lead.

The company identifies itself first with the entrepreneur, an individual who takes the initiative and acts alone. That's why we consider the idea as the first added value. The entrepreneur and the idea are intimately linked.

Very quickly, the entrepreneur can no longer act alone but in a group, within an organization of a particular nature for the common purpose of production and to sell goods and services. The problem of coherence then arises. To find coherence, it is necessary to bring people closer together, to federate. The entrepreneur's vision, then becomes their vision.

Being an entrepreneur means being a leader. It is indeed necessary as an entrepreneur to get people to follow you as you realize your project. This applies not only to customers but also to investors, banks, partners, and employees. You have to be able to lead.

It is therefore interesting to define leadership, the capacity inherent in the leader. We can define it as having influential authority based on the relationships the leader establishes with the members of a group. Therefore, being a leader is a form of recognition.

Leadership is also the process by which a person influences a group of people to achieve a common goal.[9]

We find in these two definitions the approach of bringing together a set of people for the purpose of reaching a goal.

A good leader has the humility to know that she or he is nothing without the support of others. This doesn't mean that she or he cannot accomplish big things, but it does mean that she or he is smart enough to realize that

---

[9] Peter Northhouse, *Leadership: Theory and Practice* (India: Sage, 2009).

with others, she or he can accomplish things on a broader scale. A leader opens this door of sharing, respect, and knowledge, leading to a real foundation that allows people to dream big.

As a leader you need followers. Here I would prefer the term *believers*, the ones who think about the project and who either know something or bring something to make it succeed. We've all seen brilliant people who lack charisma and the ability to share and explain smart and interesting views in a way that that connects with the audience. When you have a project, you need to carry it through, to shoulder the responsibility; you need to believe in what you want and what you can achieve in order to make others believe in your project or simply in you.

How can you expect people to believe in you if you do not first believe in yourself?

It sounds easy and even obvious, but drive is the first thing I look for when I meet a client. Sometimes people do not even know or see it in themselves, but they are inspired, and that is how they are able to inspire others.

This does not mean that they are all about themselves, explaining how good and exceptional they are. They may be shy and introverted, but when they are in their arena[10], talking about their companies or their projects, their faces lights up. They know that there is value in their projects; they trust in them or deeply believe in them.

When I see that in a client, I know that the project may or may not work, but that it will happen and it could be a great journey.

In a way, it is quite logical because without this light or this drive, people would not be able to put in as much effort as they do to build a team and inspire others to invest in them.

---

[10] Reference to the Ted Talk called The Power of Vulnerability from Brenée Brown, *"If you're not in the arena also getting your ass kicked, I'm not interested in your feedback"*.

CHAPTER 2
SUMMARIZE THE ACTIVITY

When you are considering offering a product or a service, you need to know if it has a market.

It is necessary to know if people want to buy your idea, your product, or your service. Then you should seek to satisfy an existing need. Does what you are hoping to market improve people's lives? If so, then there is an identifiable need for it.

The goal then is to define the market and your potential customers and to determine how to manage your business in the long term.

This is the time when you use creativity.

⇨ You can use drawings, videos, writings, compositions, and so forth.

You do this to effectively communicate your vision. The challenge is to move your idea out of the realm of imagination and face the intangibles.

I say to face, but more accurately, confront. This is the time when the whole first phase makes sense. If the first phase is not solid, then the second phase will take longer and be more difficult to structure or implement.

To summarize the activity, the idea must be as clear as possible. Without a clear idea, it will be impossible to present a strong, persuasive speech in two minutes. You must be convinced to convince others — hence the need to have faith in yourself and in the project.

How do you summarize and define an activity for which doubt obstructs the vision?

Well beyond having the necessary capacity to effectively synthesize the idea, you must also be prepared to confront the opinions of others. You may seek the opinions of industry professionals, various experts, friends, family, and yourself.

There is no need to get people to agree at this stage; you just need to get feedback, which could help you to structure your idea and reinforce it. At this point you want people simply to wonder, to assess, and to desire to know more. It would be even better if they then want to follow the progress of your project.

I think that the human factor is the basis of this activity, and this is the reason you need to look at others' interests. You must speak to them in the best way that you can to describe what you have in mind.

At this point, it is good to find the easiest way of picturing the implementation of your idea. It is time to let your imagination and creativity run wild.

Passionate personalities might choose to use photos or discussing their years of experience running holiday camps or in sports, for example. Pragmatists, on the other hand, will likely present numbers, their personal qualifications, and their personal experience.

At this stage the idea is not always entirely clear. Indeed, it is still liable to change in the gestation phase.

A way to begin thinking about how to make your presentation may be to ask your audience to answer the following questions:

What would you think about a service providing _____? *(describe in this space your service idea)*
Would you as a customer be interested in _____? *(describe in this space your service/ product idea)*

Questions to Ask Yourself

Is your idea really original? How so?

_____
_____
_____
_____
_____
_____
_____
_____
_____
_____
_____
_____

Why will people want to buy your product or service?

_____
_____
_____
_____
_____
_____
_____
_____
_____
_____
_____
_____

Who are your customers?

What need is your product or service filling?

Will you be able to compete with existing business? If yes, which ones?

What added value do you bring to the market? Explain.

_____
_____
_____
_____
_____
_____
_____

How will you distribute your product or provide your service? Be as precise as you can.

_____
_____
_____
_____
_____
_____
_____
_____

How will you present your product or service?

_____
_____
_____
_____
_____
_____
_____

What protection can you get for intellectual property, for example, a patent, a trademark, or a logo? (See more on this topic in chapter 5.)

_____
_____
_____
_____
_____
_____
_____
_____
_____
_____
_____
_____

Are there any governmental restrictions or obligations that could limit the use of your idea?

_____
_____
_____
_____
_____
_____
_____
_____
_____
_____
_____
_____

What resources are needed to start your business?

_____

Where can you get help in evaluating and refining your idea?

_____

After you have identified the idea, being able to summarize the activity is one important way to see if your idea is clear. As the French poet Nicolas Boileau-Despréaux said, "Whatever is well conceived is clearly said, and the words to say it flow with ease."

The next question you might have is "when is it the right moment to share your idea"? This depends on how much you want to share and with whom. This is partially a question of trust, depending on the stage of idea development that you are in, but it also be a good way for you to gauge people's initial reactions.

I have said that most of the time, people come to see me when they have become obsessed with their ideas. There is the time when you are focusing on developing the idea, looking for how to implement it, identifying your potential customer base, and so forth. The step after that is when you want to share the idea because it is turning around in your head like a hit on the radio.

Then you start to pitch. In doing so, you begin to test your idea.

I started my company by deciding to offer something useful to people. I wanted to focus on something that I knew how to do. Not being particularly skilled with my hands, I turned to an activity in which I had experience and essentially focused on what I particularly like to do. Luckily, it seemed to benefit my eventual clients and made me feel useful.

By starting to talk about my project to friends, I quickly found myself working on projects, preparing and working on business plans, negotiations, and preparations to help friends who were entrepreneurs formalize their projects. This is when I realized that I probably addressed a pain point and found something to focus on.

However, most of the time there is no point in pitching an idea if you are not able to answer basic questions like the following:

- What problem does this idea solve?
- What evidence is there that the problem is real, and important enough to solve?

- How will (or would) you solve the logistical challenges of your idea?
- Do you have a proof of concept? A prototype?
- Why are you the right person to solve this problem?
- Why should this problem be solved now?

These are good points to start with. The person pitching has usually spent some time thinking about his or her answers[11] beyond a superficial level (see chapter 6 for tips related to pitching).

---

[11] Eleazar Hernández, *Leading Creative Teams: Management Career Paths for Designers, Developers, and Copywriters* (New York: Apress, 2016), 107.

Note: Take the time to answer the preceding questions in this blank space provided or in your notebook.

CHAPTER 3

SHOW THE POTENTIAL OF THE MARKET

Understand here that we are in a mindset of making the project succeed. The goal is to consider whatever factors you can to minimize risk. Knowing the market will help to determine a target, and then we can make the most appropriate deal possible.

Questions to Initiate and Support Your Market Research

Here use a notebook to document your research so that you will later be able to analyze and summarize it, which will help you to complete or prepare your answers.

What is the target market?
_____
_____
_____
_____
_____
_____
_____
_____
_____

At what stage in the life cycle is the market (start-up, growth, maturity, decline)?

How profitable is the market? Justify your answer as well as you can.

What is its size in terms of potential revenue? Justify your answer as well as you can.

How big is this market (in value and in volume)?

What are the key distribution channels? Do the research and summarize what you find.

_____
_____
_____
_____
_____
_____
_____
_____

What is the growth rate for this market?

_____
_____
_____
_____
_____
_____
_____
_____

What are the market drivers?

_____
_____
_____
_____
_____
_____
_____
_____

Who Are My Customers?

What products or services do your potential customers want? Explain why.

_____
_____
_____
_____
_____
_____
_____
_____
_____
_____
_____
_____
_____

How would you characterize your target clients?

_____
_____
_____
_____
_____
_____
_____
_____
_____
_____
_____
_____
_____

What is the main characteristic of the target customers who will buy your product or service?

_____
_____
_____
_____
_____
_____
_____
_____
_____
_____
_____
_____
_____

What is the average income of the target customers who will buy your product or service? Justify as much as you can by mentioning your sources, for example.

_____
_____
_____
_____
_____
_____
_____
_____
_____
_____
_____
_____
_____

The Competitors

How much would customers be willing to pay for your product or service? You may consider a range of prices for your product or service.

Who are the main competitors?

Do the competitors have a competitive advantage? If yes, describe this advantage.

___

What are the barriers to entry? (Tax, environment, cost…)

___

Note: To get a better perspective on your competitors' activities and offerings, you could use a comparative table.

Questions to Ask Yourself

What are the consumer needs?
_____
_____
_____
_____
_____
_____
_____
_____
_____
_____
_____

How do your competitors talk about their deals?
_____
_____
_____
_____
_____
_____
_____
_____
_____
_____
_____

What do you most appreciate out of everything you've seen on the market?

List five key elements that best describe your competitors:

What will your product or service offer that is better than what the competition offers?

Why should customers choose your product or service over another?

Each step brings you closer to your activity and, consequently, closer to the realization of your project.

Here we begin by answering the question of feasibility of implementation of the project. This is important because it helps you to understand and focus on bringing something new to market.

The perception of the idea is important, but so is its growth and development.

One may either create a need or fill a need. A need is created when people come across something they did not know about previously because they did not have access to it. Perhaps this lack of information, technology, or knowledge is the gap that your product or service is filling in.

This is about belief and persuasion, especially when you are facing a market that is not yet in existence. In such a case, you must consider everything that may be relevant as a reference point to help you understand the market and the value of your product or service.

It is likely at this point that you will have investors interested in your project and wondering if it will be profitable. You may have even already convinced a few potential customers that the product or service that you are working on brining to market is something that they need.

This is especially important in the digital age where we often deal with new technologies, innovations and proposals that are beyond the scope of our current knowledge or experience.

For existing markets, it is important to look for figures to define the parameters of the project in the clearest, most efficient way possible. The better you understand the market, the better the chance of you entering the market successfully and making your project profitable.

Be a Strategist

The entrepreneur is a strategist because he must go through a set of processes necessary for the realization of his project. That's why leadership and strategy are intimately linked.

An entrepreneur has the following:

- ✓ an idea, a concept, a passion, an area of expertise or know-how
- ✓ a strong desire to launch
- ✓ the willingness to ask himself or herself questions
- ✓ a plan to implement his or her ideas and concepts

The objective of the market study is to better understand and know this future environment so as to be able to make better decisions upstream.

The purpose of market research for the creator of a business is to identify the expectations of future customers, their needs, the strengths and weaknesses of competitors, and also to determine the feasibility and viability of the project.

Market research entails a review of the existing market, the needs of the market, and the trends of the marketplace.

The strategy aims to outline clear goals and explain how they will be achieved. The strategist must understand the competitive forces of the industry. Otherwise, the strategy is based on luck and hope.

Once you understand the competitive environment, you must find a way to implement your idea in a way to manage these issues.

You must have an objective and a way to transform it into reality, so you will find that little by little, pragmatism replaces intuition.

The questions an entrepreneur should ask himself are as follows:

Questions to Ask in Relation to Competition

Who are the leaders in market that you are entering?

_____
_____
_____
_____
_____
_____
_____
_____
_____
_____
_____
_____
_____

How many direct competitors do you have (i.e., businesses who are doing the same thing as you're doing)?

_____
_____
_____
_____
_____
_____
_____
_____
_____
_____
_____
_____
_____

How many indirect competitors (those who provide alternatives to what you are offering) do you have?

What do you like about their offers?

How much are they willing to pay for your offer? How long do you keep your customers?

How are you improving their lives?

As a customer, would you use this product or service?

How have you felt as a customer?

What are the characteristics of successful companies and failed companies in your view?

___

What are the differentiating factors between a successful company and a failed company?

Questions to ask regarding Suppliers

Who are my potential suppliers?

How many are there?

What are their prices?

What is my bargaining power with suppliers?

Questions to ask regarding Distributors

What are the usual modes and distribution channels?

What is the cost of distribution?

Adaptability is important. Take the time to think about your strategy

In my work, I have been fortunate to work with a variety of people and companies young and old, new and established taking different approaches while sharing common traits. One that comes to my mind as I write this chapter is a company that started in France and had great success. As a result, they wished to expand abroad. The company focused on helping corporations to enhance their brands and online presence.

The founders were working on the implementation of their own presence on the Web. With their success in France, they chose to develop the same thing in Singapore. However, the market there was full of similar offerings, so the French company had more competition in Singapore than at home which led them to have to compete in a market that was much more mature and saturated.

The choice, therefore, was to change their strategy by adapting it to the market. They looked for what they could bring and what differentiated them from others.

They considered that the major point of differentiation between them and others was the fact that they were French and had chosen to develop in Asia. This led them at first to a network of French expats in Singapore. Indeed, the French have a large presence in Singapore, and the French community carries a lot of weight in the city-state of Singapore.

Moreover, based on this observation, the French company realized that many other companies would also like to take this step and that it would be beneficial for them to be able to welcome them and help them to develop in the Asian zone.

It took the founders two years to find their business model and the way to convince big companies to consider the opportunities offered to them by this French company. Today, any French entrepreneur who comes to Singapore is taken to meet one of the founders of this company. In the short space of four years, he became a key person in the start-up and innovation ecosystem of Singapore.

When you talk to the co-founder of this company about Singapore's development initiative, his words are clear: It is necessary to make sure to find the market and the customers. If the product or service does not work, there is no market. He explains openly that it was not easy to succeed in Singapore, saying that he spent two years on trying to find a place where his business was going to work. He gives very good advice and is rather open. This is the profile of an entrepreneur who does not rest but who also knows how to enjoy the good moments in life. In my opinion, this man is a good example of a successful entrepreneur in the sense that he is a smart person who knows his strengths and weaknesses. But above all, he dares to take chances.

To relate this story to the purpose of this chapter, this entrepreneur's personal qualities led him to look for market potential. Having not found a receptive market for his initial service, he explained to me that when he arrived, he networked like crazy, going to all the free seminars and even paying to attend one to get well acquainted with the local ecosystem. Once that was done, he wanted to understand the market in Singapore and discover what he could bring or what his service could bring. He realized that he was not the only one in the market and, therefore, that it was necessary to differentiate what he was offering. Today, he only works with large companies and only on projects with a value of at least six figures.

Over the next few pages, our approach will be a little bit different, using classical tools and elements to devise a marketing strategy. The goal is to allow you to choose and/or use the actual tools and analyses to get the useful information that you need.

What is this analysis for?

Before you begin to think about your strategy, your marketing mix, or even your competition, you must analyze several essential factors. Let us look at a concrete example:

While living in Asia, I had the opportunity to see a few companies arriving and dominating the new market. The interesting thing is that many of them did not stay. They finally left the market, leaving it open to other companies, sometimes a local one.

A common mistake we at my company see is that companies often use their initial business model to develop internationally without necessarily pushing too hard to understand the cultural differences or the ways in which the people of this other culture use products and services. For instance, we saw people preferring to use cash instead of a credit card in a certain country where a large global company failed to persuade potential customers to purchase their products. Their customers did not want to buy the products by entering their credit card numbers online.

We see the same situation with regard to the use of a motorbike versus a car.

A study of the environment can make a big difference in terms of market penetration. The challenges of this enterprise will be quite different from that of the Western model. Start-ups must therefore consider the whole environment.

- Is the population sensitive to the proposed product or service? (the sociocultural factor)
- Is the marketing of this product or service legal in this country? (labor laws, e-commerce, license market activity open to foreigners, and so forth)
- Is the technology that is used for this product or service used supported in this country?
- To what extent does the political environment interfere with the economy and the market for your offer?

Some people will be quite familiar with the tool I will present. I also know that others may find it very new and helpful, especially in the early stages of a company, when equipping oneself to understand the market is key.

It is a wonderful thing to present, explain, and ultimately pitch your product or service.

Understanding the Environment of the Sector (STEEPLE Analysis)

Francis Aguilar, a professor at Harvard Business School and an expert in strategy and management, is the creator of this strategic analysis technique. In his book *Scanning the Business Environment*, published in 1967, Aguilar mentions a technique for studying the environment in which a company operates. He mentions the acronym ETPS, for economic, technical, political, and social.

Later, in the 1980s, other authors[12] used the same letters but in a different order, then proposing other variations, including PESTEL, introducing the ecological notion and legal dimensions, and STEEPLE, including ethics.

The use

The tool is used to analyze the macro-environmental factors (an analysis of the external environment) that influence your company. Before any strategic decision is made, all the facets must be evaluated. You want to introduce a new product, enter a new market, and even start your own business? Then the analysis of these influencing factors must be performed to establish your marketing strategy.

PESTEL is an acronym for the following environmental factors:

Politics (political situation, market regulations, trade agreements, restrictions, lobbying, etc.)

Economic (currency rate fluctuations, GDP created by demand, tax policy, price changes, etc.)

Social (structure of population, traditions, level of education, competition, etc.)

---

[12] L. Fahey, V. Narayanan, J. Morrison, W. Renfro, W. Boucher, and M. Porter introduced the acronym PEST.

Technological (new technologies, capacity for innovation, etc.)

Environmental (pollution, environmental protection legislation, clean air and water, etc.)

Legal (tax restrictions, export and import restrictions, country tax code, fiscal policy, etc.)

Each point of the PESTEL analysis should be analyzed. They are all closely linked.

For example, a political change (P) will influence legal (L), environmental (E), economic (E), or even technological (T) factors.

The market in which your company wants to establish itself must be analyzed before you think about how to enter the market.

You can go farther with this tool by analyzing additional elements such as ethical factors, involving duty, morality, integrity, and behavior, to better understand employees and society as a whole and how these things could affect your business.

Understanding Your Environment (SWOT Analysis)

A SWOT analysis combines an internal analysis and an external analysis of your strengths, weaknesses, opportunities, and threats.

The SWOT analysis is one of the most widely used marketing tools to define a company's positioning in a given market and to define a more or less long-term strategic vision.

It is commonly accepted that the creator of the model was Albert Humphrey, while working on a Stanford University research project in the early 1960s. The goal of his work was to understand why business planning often failed. The first model developed was called SOFT ("What is good in the present is Satisfactory, good in the future is an Opportunity; bad in the present is a Fault and bad in the future is a Threat"). It was only in 1964 that the acronym SWOT appeared.

The use

This market anaylsis tool is essential to launch a product or service in a given market. It also aims to inform decision-making and define a company's strategic orientation.

Consequently, the SWOT analysis must be clear, explicit, and above all coherent. Hence, the need to select, clarify, and analyze a body of precise information and data, the source of which must be reliable.

The SWOT matrix is divided into two parts to study first, the external diagnosis, which includes the study of the market and the external environment of the company, then the internal diagnosis or the strengths and weaknesses of the company.

It is about targeting and studying positive variables on different scales:

- The environment is studied so as to make the most of it.

- Threats and weaknesses are carefully identified and analyzed to minimize risks.

Finally, the balance sheet, represented in the form of a double-entry table, is a synthesis of the market and the environment in which the company operates. This document is usually one page long (remember, it should be clear and precise). Rigor and pragmatism are the keywords in this exercise. Indeed, the SWOT lists only five or six essential elements.

To carry out your marketing study, probe the needs and expectations of your market.

With SMART Goals

SMART is an acronym that you can use to guide your goal setting. The criteria are commonly attributed to Peter Drucker's Management by Objectives concept. The first-known use of the term occurred in the November 1981 issue of *Management Review* by George T. Doran.

Since then, Professor Robert S. Rubin (Saint Louis University) wrote about SMART in an article for the Society for Industrial and Organizational Psychology. He stated that SMART has come to mean different things to different people, as shown below:

Specific (simple, sensible, significant)

So you have to ask yourself: What do I want to accomplish? Why is this goal important? Who is involved? Where will the business be located? Which resources or limits are involved?

Measurable (meaningful, motivating)

How much? How many? How will I know when it is accomplished?

Achievable (agreed, attainable)

How can I accomplish this goal? How realistic is the goal based on other constraints, such as financial factors?

Relevant (reasonable, realistic and resourced, results-based)

Does this seem worthwhile? Is this the right time? Does this match our other efforts/needs? Am I the right person to reach this goal? Is it applicable to the current socioeconomic environment?

Time-bound (time-based, time-limited, time- or cost-limited, timely, time-sensitive)

When? What will I be able to do six months from now? What will I be able to do six weeks from now? What can I do today?

The SMART indicator results from the precision of the objective set. Indeed, if the objective is not clear enough, it is impossible to verify whether it has been achieved. It is therefore essential to take the time to formulate precisely, as a group or with other people in charge of the project, the objectives so that the implementation of these indicators is as optimal as possible.

Case Study: Tennis School SWOT Example

Now, let's look at the example of a client who wanted to build a tennis school from scratch in Asia. His name is William. Starting as a student in tennis school at the age of fourteen his passion for tennis quickly grew and he played in amateur tournaments. After few years he became a certified instructor.

William did his training in England, at the Federal Tennis School, under the tutelage of a professional tennis player. He decided after his certification to practice professionally in Asia. Thus, he started to work as a tennis coach in 2011 and is now the founder of a tennis school in Asia.

He offers different packages designed for any type of player, from beginners to advanced players, adults and children.

The frequency of lessons is calculated and organized so that the students' learning and progress will be as fast as possible.

STRENGTHS
- **Quality** of the training.
- **The place:** The classes will take place in a five stars hotel.
- **Certified instructor**
- **Method:** Already tried and proofed.
- **Clients** already interrested
- **Experience in Asia** as coach and instructor since 2011
- **Network and support from professional** tennis player

WEAKNESSES
- **The trainer will be alone** to train his students at the beginning
- **The time** to train and recruit other instructor
- **The image of the company** need to be build
- **The legal structure** will evoluate
- **Lack of experience** in managing a company
- **The context** in Asia regarding the activity as a foreigner
- **The finance** (small budget)

OPPORTUNITIES
- **Potential investors and partners:** Few investors who already tryied the method expressed their interested in the project
- **The director of the venue** accepted to implement the project in their hotel
- **The project can be duplicate**
- **The return on investment** can be fast
- It is an **emerging market**

THREATS
- **Management Capacity** of the company
- **The legal context**
- **The development of the market** can be slower than our forecast
- **New competitors**

Model of SWOT

CHAPTER 4

STRUCTURE YOUR BUSINESS

After reading the three previous chapters, you now determine that the structure needs a backbone.

Some will be more comfortable than others with going faster and will complete some of the steps in one go.

However, based on our experience, it is best to separate each step, which will allow you to see your progress with regard to the project.

Structuring the idea will help you to establish an action plan and will enable you to see clearly what your needs are for the proper implementation of your project.

Many ideas do not get beyond the idea stage while others collapse before they are achieved. The structuring phase allows you to get a more concrete idea.

This part is the analysis and reconciliation, and therefore the structure, of the past three steps.

Answer the following questions:

Who are your prospects?

Where will you approach them, and how?

What will you tell them?

What is your idea? How will you present it?

Why will they listen to you?

When will you put your idea into practice?

With all this information, you may be able to write your marketing plan.

Marketing is a key element of business success. You need to decide which customers to target. You must consider how you will reach new customers and win them over. You must ensure that existing customers remain satisfied. You must also continue to review and improve what you do in order to stay ahead of the competition.

Your marketing plan should be the reference document used as a base to run your marketing strategy. It sets clear objectives and explains how you will reach your clients. Perhaps most importantly, it is a study to discover how you can ensure that your plan becomes reality.

The marketing plan will use the tools presented in the previous chapter, summarizing and analyzing the research already done.

> Remember that marketing in itself will not guarantee sales, but by adopting a well-researched and coherent plan, you are more likely to reinforce your credibility.

What if the Market Doesn't Exist?

Everything depends on the need. If there is a market, there is a target. If there is a target, there is a need, a problem, or a hope. Therefore, if the need does not exist, neither does the market.

However, we can always create an innovative product and business model by creating new uses or new habits, or expand existing markets with new targets. To create an innovative product, we may invent a new way of doing something to satisfy a need, simplify the solution to a problem, or solve a new problem. A product of this nature may be profitable, but the beginnings can be difficult. It sometimes takes time for a sufficient number of customers to become interested enough in your innovation to buy your product. To create an innovative business model, you may modify the way of distributing a product or service, modify the way your customers pay, or modify the place of distribution of your product or service. Airbnb is a good example of creating a new use or a new habit. Examples of expanding existing markets with new targets include the sports market, which has opened up to seniors as customers, and the drone market, whose target has moved beyond the military market to open up to individuals.

In the validation process for a project, the market study may focus on the acceptability of the product or service through the use of quantitative or qualitative data, or it may be more oriented toward measuring the potential of a market with the use of statistical data relating to consumer behavior and available geo-marketing data (documentary studies).

The first thing to do is to document the market you want to enter. First, several questions will have to be answered.

To find all this information, refer to the literature in your area of specialization, professional databases (like Xerfi), and articles and websites that deal with the subject. The idea is to understand the workings and key characteristics of the targeted market. Once you have answered all these questions, you will have a different vision.

You must have a clear understanding of the challenges of the market in which you want to operate. You understand that if it is a niche market, the implementation strategy will not be the same as for a large market with many prospects and competitors. You should not miss a thing!

The Value Proposition

A **value proposition** is a business or marketing statement that a company uses to summarize why a consumer should buy a product or use a service. This statement convinces a potential consumer that one particular product or service will add more **value** or better solve a problem than other, similar offerings.

The value proposition helps to build your credibility and your brand. (You may have already covered this in the questionnaire in chapter 2.)

Value creation: what, and for whom?

It is important to understand your business, which might sound obvious, but it is a long process. Basically, having an understanding of the interest of each stakeholder is a good start. This is the reason why we wonder what the benefits are to our shareholders. They are all looking for something. Considering the benefits created by your business for them will bring a different angle in terms of thinking about and developing the value proposition.

Who	Benefits
Shareholder	Shareholder value => value of the share and dividends
Employees	Salary upgrading and profit sharing
Customers	Product with high added value
State	Value added tax, profits and capital gains
Banks	Interest on debt financing investments and working capital

Who benefits?

How is value created within the company?

The creation of value results from a company's capacity to achieve at best a junction between the field of knowledge and the needs, expectations, and dreams of its potential customers by offering a creative line of products or services that are manufactured efficiently, well distributed, and available at a price that is in direct proportion to the amount of satisfaction provided.

This is what the image below shows.

- The creative genius of individuals
- Progress in knowledge, science and technology
- The ability to create products and services that meet the needs of society
- The industrial engineering that is to produce them in a scientific and organized way, in quality, quantity and low cost
- Free competition, which ensures the constant optimization of the industrial system according to best practices and its renewal due to the dynamism of new entrants
- An open distribution system allowing free access of individuals to all products and services by the market

Creation of value

Even if the value created is generally measured in financial terms, it is essentially based on non-financial items. It results from the dynamics of the skill set. The creation of absolute value can be assessed only according to the best available offer, which must consider the state of competition.

The project is the only way to stimulate and combine potentially divergent interests, which only harmonize when there is a common future goal.

We at 8S2Business often attend pitch sessions, which are very interesting for many reasons. We will focus here on the start-up pitch, which is presented in business plan contests or in sessions with incubators or accelerators.

Start-up companies or entrepreneurs seem to be regularly seeking funds and consequently need to convince those to whom they are pitching. However, the presentations that they make most of the time do not really show the value that they will be bringing to the lives of their consumers. Some focus on the quality of the technology they are using more than on the users.

The approach always surprises me. I can see that some of them try very hard to convince the audience of the quality of their tool because of its complexity, while they don't say much about how they will make money from the product or discuss the reasons that customers will choose their product over another.

When you are pitching to raise funds, you must be serious about building your business. This is where the business plan becomes crucial, along with a business model to help your audience understand the value your product or service will be creating.

This is the reason why in the context of the business plan or pitch, we can observe frustration both in the person interested in investing and the person looking for funding for his or her new company.

If at some point you seek investment in your project and to create a business with it, you must show how your business will be feasible, viable, and economically sustainable.

One of the causes of this frustration is probably related to how each party perceives the other, but we will come back to this point in chapter 6.

The Business Model

A simple question sums up everything: How will you make money?

The company must be economically efficient if it is to survive. It is from this point that the company derives its ability to create value. However, this creation of value is never guaranteed.

The company's survival depends on the business model, but it is a fragile and complex process to find or build one that works. Moreover, there is no guarantee that a company that created a lot of value in the past will continue its performance in the future.

How to Summarize the Hypothesis

Alex Osterwalder[13] has developed the "business model canvas," which is essentially an organized way to lay out your assumptions clearly.

The Business Model Canvas

Following is a table inspired by the business model canvas:

Partners	Activities	Resources	Value Proposition	Customer relationship	Chanel	Customer segments
	Cost				Revenue	

Business model

---

[13] Strategyzer, https://www.strategyzer.com/canvas.

Case Study: Start with the non-scalable

I will take the example of Jim, who used to work in marketing for a big company developing its business in Asia. In his job, Jim had to arrange spaces for retail stores. Thanks to his position, he had the opportunity to work in the luxury industry. After ten years, he felt comfortable enough to launch his own company.

The company was based on selling an application allowing stores to get perfume through a connected diffuser and managed through a platform. Jim thought that the scalability of his business would be easy thanks to the technology.

Like many first-time entrepreneurs using new technologies, Jim, feeling that he had the advantage of a powerful engine that worked by itself and focused more on the technology than on the service it provided, the value that it added, the need it addressed, or on the consumer.

After building the application, and despite his background in marketing, Jim struggled in the running of his company. He realized that to make it work, he needed to curate and build the list of perfumes. Moreover, he needed to get paying customers for his product.

Even though we know that a tech product can go viral, it is really important for people who wish to start a business in this industry to realize that before being scalable, most of the big, successful companies started by addressing the non-tech and non-scalable part to develop the product and better address the needs of the target market.

In the end the user will be the one who will make your application a success. The focus needs to be on the user, so at the beginning you need to go and get the user on board.

The business model allows the business owner to understand the business itself, its needs, its source of revenue, its value proposition, its market, and its customers.

It is useful to create a business model when you start your business, but you should also create one when you are thinking about launching a new product with an existing company, for example. The reasons for this are similar, such as giving you the benefit of clarity when you are working on your idea. It is important to see the difference between building a project and building a business.

We have worked with a number of companies developing tech products. The recurring situation we observed was the unwillingness to connect with customers physically, to meet the client or other stakeholders and talk to them to better understand their needs and, most importantly, why it made sense for them to use the product.

Another example is a company that wanted to use influencers to promote the sale of its products, but they had no idea about the potential impact on the people in the region they wanted to launch their product in. They also had no clue about how to reach these people or the end consumers. One of our recommendations was that they highlight the fact that they needed to meet some influencers or agencies to learn more about these things, but that for them was a no go, even when we proposed to do it for them. They just wanted to avoid it. Since they were working in data analysis, they decided to use the data to get their own opinions on the situation, but there were still so many unknowns.

They did not want to push the matter any farther as it started to look like a lot of work. Simply put, they did not feel comfortable about continuing. They decided to postpone the realization of this project, which indeed stayed at the project stage even though the idea was a good one.

This is the difference between a long-term business projection and a short-term business view, or the difference between a project and a business, as mentioned earlier.

Most of time, the execution and the capacity to set the project in motion are crucial. When your business is ongoing and you basically use new technologies, one of your keys to succeed is to invent and reinvent to improve both your product and the lives of your users.

CHAPTER 5

SELECT YOUR LEGAL FORM

Probably because of my legal background, I think that compliance research needs to happen as soon as possible in the life of the project. It frames things in a real-world context and helps to address critical issues early.

The principle of innovation is its newness. And we know that the society is developing faster than the law. Because of this, you may encounter gray areas or wavering, so you had better be prepared.

When we are talking about legal form, we are also speaking more generally about standards, licensing, authorization, qualifications, and things of that ilk.

At this stage it is important to be aware of all the necessary authorizations, their costs, what is required to set up, and the time needed to do so.

This part is not the sexiest part for entrepreneurs. It can at times be a little sloppy, or it may be postponed due to a lack of knowledge in the field or the cost of going to see a lawyer. Still, it remains an extremely important and helpful component following the development of the project.

Once the legal framework is laid down, the guidelines emerge by themselves. What remains to be done is the merely checking off the boxes on your to-do list to be sure that you do not forget anything.

This step allows marks the turning point leading to the drafting of your business plan.

At this point, the opinion of a professional can be decisive and help you avoid errors and unpleasant surprises, which could cost much more.

We will present here a few points for you to consider. The goal really is to create awareness more than replace the advice of a professional. Remember also that the solution proposed or used by your friends or other entrepreneurs is not necessarily the best one for you.

Secure your development: Minimize the risk or calculate it

The example we are going to use here is that a French company, a start-up that already enjoyed great success due to its product. The technology of this product allowed the company to file patents, raise funds, and win awards on an international scale.

This start-up wished to develop in Asia. Not having the necessary funds and no knowledge on the ground, they agreed to use an exclusive distributor with whom they had been in discussions for two years.

So, three years later, the launch was done by the distributor's company, which was registered, but only for the purpose of exclusively distributing this product. The problem was that shortly after launching all the marketing campaigns, both companies realized that they did not quite see things the same way.

Indeed, some grey areas had been left for later discussion, which had not occurred before the launch of the product in Asia. Therefore, the exclusive distributor, whose name was not even thought of to develop any other brands but this one, had not seen or signed a contract to develop the market. The company had started all that with a gentleman's agreement. Once the investors of the Asian company realized this, they felt that they were all freewheeling. What could possibly go wrong?

The French start-up, who wanted an exclusive distributor who would take all the risks for the development of the brand in the area, could leave at any time, retaining the right to extract themselves without having to lose anything in the process and without having to justify their actions or inaction.

As you can imagine, a long discussion ensued, but the situation of the exclusive distributor was becoming more and more uncomfortable. Two years later, the distributor decided to end the collaboration despite a very big opportunity in the region. The distributor had recovered most of the initial investment, but the relationship ended, and the negotiation stopped.

This situation of fighting for the exclusive right to distribute is what put the noose around the neck of the distributor, for whom the goals were literally impossible to reach, especially during the first year. The penalty for this was the end of the contract and that the consequence, in addition to the shortfall, was the loss of the startup costs and time.

So, secure your project as much as you can and calculate the risk that you are taking.

Legal System Overview

It is important to be aware of your legal obligations in order to be sure that you are able to start doing business.

Indeed, this part involves considering one of the important parts of your initial investment, so prepare for that in order to be ready.

This is the part where we see if the entrepreneur has done his or her homework, that is, the research leading to secures his or her business, his or her investment, and his or her investors (if any).

It is an asset in terms of credibility if you are already able to show that you have covered the legal aspects and options, which would affect the structure of the business and startup capital needed.

Regarding the legal system,[14] it is this that sets the framework of the business.

First you must determine if the activity you are proposing is legal.

Here we can take the example of a famous company described as an "American multinational transportation network company (TNC) offering services that include peer-to-peer ridesharing, ride service hailing, food delivery, and a bicycle-sharing system. This San Francisco–based company has operations in 785 metropolitan areas worldwide. Its platforms can be accessed via its websites and mobile apps."[15]

The company struggled to develop its market in Europe particularly because of the regulations and the powerful taxi driver lobbies. We all can see here the importance of considering the legal system and the necessity of being ready to confront it with time and money if you want to change the status quo.

Next you must ask how you can structure your business based on your actual and future needs.

Will you be able to have all the authorizations straightaway, or do you prefer to proceed in phases to be able to finance your company or to develop your structure and activity?

To cover the first point, look at the economic situation and the relevant political institutions. The goal is to know who is in charge. In front of which institution do you need to appear to ask for your authorization, license, etc.?

Check with the legal and judicial system to get a general view of the way the legal system works.

---

[14] A legal system is a procedure or process for interpreting and enforcing the law.
[15] Wikipedia, s.v. "Uber," last modified May 20, 2020, https://en.wikipedia.org/wiki/Uber.

Investment

There are different ways to invest in a company.

Honestly, the focus can be on money, for obvious reasons, but think also of friends, family, and other people you know who would be keen to help you, perhaps offering you space in their office or giving you tables, chairs, or computers to allow you to work. Do not underestimate this type of support.

> An investment is an asset or item acquired with the goal of generating income or appreciation. In an economic sense, an investment is the purchase of goods that are not consumed today but are used in the future to create wealth.
>
> In finance , an investment is a monetary asset purchased with the idea that the asset will provide income in the future or will later be sold at a higher price for a profit.[16]

Always look at the prohibitions and restrictions in terms of investment in order to be ready to grow wisely and avail yourself of the full opportunity to raise money later.

Incorporating

There are typically only a few options for how you structure your company. Even if you are growing your company and you have the option to change its structure later, it will cost you money, but a solution can be found.

However, understanding your needs will help you to select the structure that best meets them and supports your development plan.

---

[16] James Chen, "Investment," Investopedia, last modified February 27, 2020, https://www.investopedia.com/terms/i/investment.asp.

When you register your company, the type of corporation you chose is important in terms of the liability and limitation of responsibility for the director(s). The best choice of corporation type is also based on what you aim to do with your company. Important considerations are the number of staff members you want to have, the number of directors and investors, the tax you will need to pay (personal or corporate), and so forth.

Get advice from a professional to be sure that you have all the information you need to register your company, however it is structured, and to ensure the company will be strong enough to grow based on the type of corporation.

Employment

It is very important to be aware of the labor framework. Growing your company involves hiring people such as interns, assistants, and accountants.

Knowing the regulations, you can write a contract outlining the terms and conditions of work, which, as you can imagine, are just the basics.

At the very beginning of your activity, you may not find it necessary to hire a specialized HR professional, but as soon as you start or grow quickly and need to hire a lot of people, human resources will become a real concern. Hiring and managing your hires can be time-consuming and difficult, particularly at the end of a labor contract.

Intellectual Property

Intellectual property is an asset for any company. More than protecting all the things that need to be protected, you also need to calculate the cost of getting this protection and to ensure that you will be able to protect your company against any infringement. Indeed, to protect your assets will cost you a lot of money.

This is actually a point that many people do not mention, but it costs a great deal to protect intellectual property assets. In some businesses, video game companies for example, protecting your intellectual property is even more important. It would be a bad idea to avoid spending money on a patent, in such a case.

Indeed, the cost of twenty years' protection may not be really necessary or relevant for a product with a life span and a return on investment within the first six months or the first year of launch, where the technology is quickly changing or evolving.

In other cases, like that of the pharmaceutical industry, where inventions and development take time and where other companies may make use of the product, the position is the opposite, so an intellectual property strategy is a real need. It is, in this case, an integral part of the business.

The point here is to consciously be sure that you have a full understanding, or at least a good understanding, of a certain product as an asset to your company.

Not everything can be protected, so do your research and get relevant advice to get the full picture of your asset in order to use it and protect it as best you can.

National and international Intellectual Property organizations are a good start.[17] They are generally keen to explain the cost to you and the process of getting the protection you need. On top of that, an intellectual property lawyer can help you to build a stronger intellectual property strategy if you are seeking to develop and distribute worldwide.

---

[17] For example WIPO, which can be found online here: https://www.wipo.int/portal/en/index.html. Also useful is the INPI in France: https://www.inpi.fr/fr, and the IPOS in Singapore, https://www.ipos.gov.sg/.

Questions to Ask Yourself

What business structure should I choose?

Where should I register?

Does my company meet all the conditions for the structure I have chosen?

List here the requirements you need to fulfill to open your company (IDs, proof of address, social capital, shareholder agreement, etc.). Get the advice of a professional to be sure you have all the right information.

Do I need an operating license? An export license? An import license?

Do I have all the credentials I need to practice or operate?

Do I need a visa or a residency permit? (If you have an international business structure, this is especially important information to know.)

If yes, how can I get one? How long will it take?

CHAPTER 6

SUGGEST A FINANCIAL PLAN

The financial plan dictates how you will finance your project.

If you need a loan or capital from investors, or both, thanks to your having convinced others with your business plan, the financial plan will serve to delineate the different contributions and where the funds will come from according to the funding requirements already in place.

The core elements of the financial plan are:

- ✓ operating margin—operating profit / turnover
- ✓ growth rate of revenue per year
- ✓ percent of sales by product line
- ✓ net margin—net income / turnover
- ✓ gross margin
- ✓ salary
- ✓ turnover

The financial plan consists of at least one of the following:

- ✓ income statement
  The income statement is the "movie" of your activity. It traces the products and resources, and the costs and expenses of the activity between two dates.
- ✓ cash flow plan
  This helps you to establish a monthly statement of available cash and the expenses you need to support.

The financial plan will enable investors to calculate their return on investment based on your project profitability indicators.

The following are a few simple tables that will allow you to bring some tangible information to your presentation.

Start-Up Costs

Start-Up Costs	Actual	Budgeted
Accounting services		
Advertising and promotion for opening		
Architectural design		
Cash		
Decorating		
Deposits for utilities		
Equipment		
Estimated taxes		
Headhunting or other hiring costs		
Installation of equipment		
Insurance		
Legal costs		
Licenses and permits		
Moving costs		
Office supplies		
Print design		
Printing		
Remodeling, build-out		
Rent deposits		
Salaries		
Signs		
Software		
Starting inventory		
Unanticipated expenses		
Vehicles		
Website		
Other		
Total start-up costs		

Income Statement

Simplified Income Statement (Dollars) (Year 1 to 3)			
Year	Year 1	Year 2	Year 3
1. Sales	$.............	$.............	$.............
2. Cost of Sales	$.............	$.............	$.............
3. Gross Margin (1-2)	$.............	$.............	$.............
4. Rent	$.............	$.............	$.............
5. AWS Hosting	$.............	$.............	$.............
6. Tech Staff (In-House/Out-Sourced)	$.............	$.............	$.............
7. Customer Service	$.............	$.............	$.............
8. Business Development	$.............	$.............	$.............
9. Admin	$.............	$.............	$.............
10. Consulting	$.............	$.............	$.............
11. Total General & Admin Costs (4 to 10)	$.............	$.............	$.............
12. EBITDA: Earnings Before Interest, Taxes, Depreciation & Amortization (3 - 11)	$.............	$.............	$.............
13. Income Tax (X%)	$.............	$.............	$.............
14. Net Income (12 - 13)	$.............	$.............	$.............

Income statement example

Balance Sheet Example

Example Company Balance Sheet December 31, 2019

ASSETS		LIABILITIES	
Current assets		**Current liabilities**	
Cash	$ 2,100	Notes payable	$ 5,000
Petty cash	100	Accounts payable	35,900
Temporary investments	10,000	Wages payable	8,500
Accounts investments	40,500	Interest payable	2,900
Inventory	31,000	Taxes payable	6,100
Supplies	3,800	Warranty liability	1,100
Prepaid insurance	1,500	Unearned revenues	1,500
Total current assets	89,000	Total current liabilities	61,000
Investments	36,000	**Long term liabilities**	
		Notes payable	20,000
Property, plant & equipment		Bond payable	400,000
Land	5,500	Total long-term liabilities	420,000
Land improvements	6,500		
Buildings	180,000	Total liabilities	481,000
Equipment	201,00		
Less: accum depreciation	(56,000)		
Prop, plant & equip - net	337,000	**STOCKHOLDERS' EQUITY**	
Intangible assets		Common stock	110,000
		Retained earnings	220,000
Goodwill	105,000	Accum other	9,000
Trade names	200,000	comprehensive income	
Total intangible assets	305,000	Less: Treasury stock	(50,000)
		Total stockholders' equity	289,000
Other assets	3,000		
		Total liabilities &	$ 770,000
Total assets	$ 770,000	stockholders' equity	

*The notes to the sample balance sheet have been omitted.

Balance sheet example

Projected Cash Flow Example

Projected Cash Flow	July '16	Aug '16	Sept '16	Oct '16	Nov '16	Dec '16
Net Cash from Operations	**$102,848**	**$426,268**	**$600,038**	**$75,493**	**$432,387**	**$436,953**
Net Profit	$135,250	$362,562	$408,182	$338,344	$248,060	$305,304
Depreciation & Amortization	$298	$297	$298	$297	$298	$298
Change in Accounts Receivable	($91,584)	($126,576)	($25,920)	$38,880	$50,544	($31,450)
Change in Inventory	($22,950)	$1,260	$2,040	$1,740	$405	$0
Change in Accounts Payable	$5,622	($2,916)	$393	($457)	($534)	$314
Change in Income Tax Payable	$33,812	$90,641	$102,045	($141,911)	$62,014	$76,327
Change in Sales Tax Payable	$42,400	$101,000	$113,000	($161,400)	$71,600	$86,160
Net Cash from Investing	**($16,000)**	**($1,000)**	**($1,000)**	**($1,000)**	**($1,000)**	**($1,000)**
Investment Received	$10,000					
Dividends and Distributions	($1,000)	($1,000)	($1,000)	($1,000)	($1,000)	($1,000)
Assets Purchased or Sold	($25,000)					
Net Cash from Financing		**($50,000)**	**($1,329)**	**($1,332)**	**($1,336)**	**($1,339)**
Change in Short-term Debt		$16,169	$40	$41	$40	$41
Change in Long-term Debt		$33,381	($1,369)	($1,373)	($1,376)	($1,380)
Cash at Beginning of Period	$0	$86,848	$562,116	$1,159,825	$1,232,986	$1,663,037
Net Change in Cash	$86,848	$475,268	$597,709	$73,161	$430,051	$434,614
Cash at End of Period	**$86,848**	**$562,116**	**$1,159,825**	**$1,232,986**	**$1,663,037**	**$2,097,651**

Cash flow table example

Are Investors in it just for money?

Everybody has a function within the company structure. Each person brings something to the table, so they are compensated with money or other rewards.

- The entrepreneur brings the idea, the vision, the expertise, and the know-how.
- The business partners bring their personal support, expertise and maybe some financial support, but also their know-how and expertise.
- The business developer brings his or her know-how regarding sales, partnerships, and other portfolios.
- The CTO[18] brings his or her expertise in building the website and the app and managing the architecture of the tech aspects of the project.
- The marketing people develop the tools to reach the client efficiently, ensuring your company has a visible presence.

Everyone involved has a specific task to perform, so understandably get money in return, in the form of either salary or stock.

We all accept and see the value and the benefits of those who support the entrepreneur in his or her work. It is not easy to imagine making these people work for free, without any rewards for their efforts.

In our experience working with start-ups, we often see early-stage companies or entrepreneurs looking for funds. They look at this more as a numbers game than as something representing know-how, the portfolio, mentoring, or consulting. However, what are you expecting from the investors, and what do you think the investor is expecting from you and your company?

Investors can be involved and interested in the company, especially in the early stages, for many reasons.

---

[18] Chief technology officer.

If you put yourself in the shoes of the investor, what would you like to see in the company you are investing in?

Of course you would like to see a return on your investment, earning money from the investment, but we all know that any money you may earn will be based on the well-being of the company and the result of work performed by the people involved in the company itself to make things happen. In other words, the amount you make will depend on the execution.

More than a wallet, investors support companies as if they were additional members of the management team, with whom they share the same goal, namely, the success of the company. They bring money, but oftentimes they bring more than that, such as their know-how, their contacts, their experience, and their ideas. This is the reason why they are paid in return.

Here we are mainly talking about angel investors because of the stage of the company we are discussing: the business start-up.

Having this information in mind, you can better understand and work differently on the presentation of the company to the people who are helping you to bring your project to fruition.

Imagine yourself as an investor, and then imagine someone is coming to you and telling you, "I need five million dollars to carry out this huge and ambitious project. I will build a chain of bars in Europe, starting with the capital and then grow based on the revenue I will get from the business. I have never run a bar, but I know well how one works as I used to go to bars a lot. I would organize parties and mixologist contests to gain visibility. My bar will be the place to be."

"Do you know where you will start?" you ask.

"I think I will start in Paris because I am French and I know the city well."

"Do you know in which quarter you will locate your bar, and the rental cost?"

"I think the third quarter. And the range of prices will be based on my research on the internet."

"Have you met any people who have agreed to work with you?"

"For the moment I have a few people who are interested in working with me, but I continue to consider people with specific skills to reinforce my idea."

"Exactly how would you use this five million dollars?"

"On hiring people, on buying or renting a place depending on which is better and the opportunities that I have."

"You should design the place online with the brand. I've already worked on it. I have a 3D design of the place that I can show you."

Let's stop the conversation here.

How would you feel investing five million dollars in this project? Are the elements here enough for you as an investor to support the project?

Most of the time, an entrepreneur will work on convincing his CTO, business partners, marketing team, and others. He will focus on being sure that he is able to pay them and giving them something concrete to allow them to leave their jobs and follow him as this new adventure unfolds. Having this credibility is very important.

It is the same for the investor, who should be credible, practical, have realistic expectations and treat the business as a serious venture to be involved with rather than a whim.

In the aforementioned imaginary discussion, a few elements are missing. These must be supplied if the entrepreneur is to reach the point where he starts to look credible.

What to know about angel investors

Many entrepreneurs wonder how to talk to investors, especially to angel investors.[19] We will point out the four points you need to consider and keep in mind if you want to be able to capture their attention. This is not an exact science, but it does serve as a useful reference point that could help you when you pitch.

The benefits you can gain, other than money, by taking on an angel investor are as follows:

- ✓ Contacts with venture capitalists and strategic partners, lawyers, bankers, accountants, and investment bankers
- ✓ Introductions to potential customers or employees
- ✓ Advice and counsel
- ✓ Credibility by being endorsed by the investor
- ✓ Knowledge of the marketplace and of the strategies of similar companies

Most angel investors invest between $25,000 and $100,000 in a company on average. The three important things an angel investor will consider are as follows:

- ✓ The quality, passion, commitment, and integrity of the founder(s)
- ✓ The market opportunity being addressed and the potential for the company to become very big
- ✓ A clearly thought out business plan, and any early evidence of the plan's gaining traction

Before talking to any investor, you need to anticipate a few questions, such as "How much capital are you hoping to raise?"

---

[19] Richard Harroch, "20 Things All Entrepreneurs Should Know about Angel Investors," *Forbes*, February 5, 2015, https://www.forbes.com/sites/allbusiness/2015/02/05/20-things-all-entrepreneurs-should-know-about-angel-investors/3/#2e24415f1acb.

Think about how to justify the amount by projecting ahead for the next two years and explaining how long the capital will last.

You also may explain the key cost components and highlight your gross margins to allow the potential investors to get an idea of your business model. This helps them to better understand when and how you will make money and also what you will need to do so.

When your company is in the early stages, the valuation is always a tricky question for you as an entrepreneur. How can you place a value on a company that does not yet exist or on an activity that is not yet happening?

Well, as you can imagine, a few others have made these same observations but succeeded in getting support nevertheless.

At this stage the valuation is determined by negotiations, but a few factors remain essential:

- **Your team**

The experience and past success of your team is important. Present your team, and explain who you all are. Potential investors would like to think that you know what you are doing or at least that you have the resources to make it happen.

- **Market knowledge and analysis**

Potential investors need to see and understand the market opportunity, the competitive environment, your position, and the conditions that must be met to penetrate the market.

It sounds obvious, but if you do not have a market, then it also means you have no customers.

Most entrepreneurs in the early stages of their businesses like to think and say that they do not have any competition. This is quite common and presented as something to highlight the uniqueness of the product. However, people do not necessarily realize that if there seems to be no competition, it could be because no one is interested in the product or the service. (No customer → no market → no business.) So simply finding no competition is not everything; you should drill down on the reason why.

- **The investment conditions**

Show that you value the support of your investors who will be part of the adventure and the team.

However, if things go wrong or if, in the process of growing your company undergoes some changes, show your prospective investors the exit potential.

Sadly, despite all your efforts to make it work, we all know that the great majority of prospective investors are likely to reject you.

Here are the most common reasons why investors reject an investment opportunity:

- ✓ The market opportunity or potential size of the business is perceived as too small.
- ✓ The founders don't come across as knowledgeable or passionate.
- ✓ The sector that the start-up will be operating in is not of interest to the investor.
- ✓ The risk of losing their investment is too great

How to Pitch

By way of pitching your idea, you embody it, which becomes obvious for the one who pitches and therefore for the one who hears the pitch too.

Having attended many start-up presentations to investors, I believe that this section is essential throughout the development of the company but also after the company has been established. This has also been confirmed through the workshops that I propose or the business plan competitions that my company organizes. Pitching is an exercise which most people unfamiliar with but which is useful to them in the framework of networking. You must understand networking and conceive of it as a tool that will serve you permanently, even if you adapt it to pertain specifically to your audience.

In the context of entrepreneurs, the exercise is relevant when talking to customers, investors, and potential partners at every stage of the company's development. For start-ups, this is illustrated in the context of competitions, where the principals are asked to present their company in two, three, five, or ten minutes.

Although the exercise is excellent, it is not simple. You must capture the attention and interest of the person in front of you within the first minute of the interview.

As you know, or as you will soon come to know, the pitch is very important for entrepreneurs, so you must be good at it. Pitch everybody all the time. Pitch your mother, your father, your sister, your friends, your cousins, and so forth. The more you pitch, the better you will be at it.

Make it a goal to be able to pitch as if you were introducing yourself, giving your name, date of birth, and address in a natural and obvious way. Own it!

By providing training on the subject, I have come to the realization that some people are more comfortable with pitching than others, but overall, very few people describe pitching as easy. Some have been helped by spending years in the theater but lost it when they were put in a contest situation where they had to deliver an eloquent pitch. I've seen others hide themselves behind their shyness to justify a poor presentation, saying that it is not for them.

On the other hand, it is common among entrepreneurs to work on their projects so much that the synthesis becomes more and more complicated. They want to say everything, giving details that might be irrelevant or too precise to keep the interest of the person listening.

Here are some elements that a successful pitcher should integrate:

- The greater the mastery of the subject, the easier it is for the person who is pitching. The first thing to do is to **work, work, work**! The pitch must be prepared to sound as natural as possible. It may seem contradictory, but this is a necessary step to convey your idea and show that you know what you are talking about.

- **Use simple words** that speak to everyone, even to those who are unfamiliar with the subject.

- **Look at the people you talk to**, no matter how many of them there are. Try to connect with your audience. Do not focus too much on your sheet of notes, your PowerPoint presentation, or your shoes.

- **Smile**, be positive and happy to share with others. You are part of a gathering of people you're hoping to form relationships with, so it is essential not to give the impression of being austere or uninterested in your audience. In fact, if you fail to smile, be positive, and be happy to share, then your potential investors will lose interest in you at best or have a bad image of you at worst.

- **Remember that** you are talking about a service or a product, but especially that **you are talking to someone**. Do not overdo it, but strike a balance so that you do not seem to be apologizing for being there.

Some Common and Practical Tips

- **Ask people a common** enough **question** to connect with as many of them as you can, such as, "Who among you has ever been confronted with stage fright? Or the fear of speaking in public? Or presenting vital information?" Or "Do you know the number of people infected by the AIDS virus per hour in the world?" Of course, this last question must be closely related to your topic to make a full impact.

- **Explain the needs of your customers** and simply describe the problem that you are proposing to solve, even if the subject is complex. Popularize your remarks so that it is obvious and clear to non-specialists too.

- **Present your offering with a few keywords**, showing why you are interested in what you are going to be talking about.

- **Send a clear message.** Put forward your essential message. If there were only one thing to remember, what would it be?

- **Tell a story** to sell a dream and showcase your product or solution, a bit like politicians or leaders do. Use pictorial terms; make allegories and use metaphors.

- Do not talk too fast, and pay attention to your movements. Adapt your body language. *Use yourself.* You are your best ambassador.

I've often noticed in start-up contests that it is not always the best product that wins but the best pitch. In real life presentations to investors, this is also quite common. This justifies all the interest in the subject and the corresponding literature.

If there were six points I'd like you to remember, I would say that you should focus on the following:

- presence
- enthusiasm

- commitment
- passion
- confidence
- authenticity

Five Tips to Convince Others in Two Minutes

When you meet up with a partner or an investor, or when you participate in a networking event or an interview, it's important to introduce yourself efficiently.

Be simple.
This sounds easy, but the simplest things are the hardest to do. Use simple but powerful words to generate curiosity and make people to want to know more about you.

Be relevant.
Your speech should be structured. Talk about yourself and your project using keywords. Take the time to prepare your speech.

Be confident.
Show your originality, including why you are different and reliable in your work. Make your audience trust you.

Be ready to convince.
Be sure of what you're saying if your hope is to convince your audience. If you don't remember your speech or if you feel uncomfortable, ask questions. In this way, you show your interest in your discussion partner.

Smile.
Your audience will welcome your speech.

CHAPTER 7

SET UP YOUR BUSINESS PLAN

The business plan is the part where the project begins to become concrete. The quality of the business plan will depend on how much attention you have paid to the previous steps.

It is important to understand that at all stages of the life of a company, the business plan will not be the same. It will change over time, but you still need a basis to start from. This exercise may seem restrictive, but undeniably it will allow you to give structure to your ideas.

In her enthusiasm, an entrepreneur may be carried away by her project, which can be fatal in terms of implementation. It can cause the people on the project to cease performing their work. It can hinder investment or the feasibility of the project, perhaps in terms of the launch. On the contrary, if the entrepreneur remains focused, this reinforces the fact that the whole project is quite feasible.

The business plan can be either a boost or a drag.

It is important to understand that this is also the place where it pays to get help.

> **The exercise may seem restrictive, but it allows to structure the ideas for the entrepreneurs and the other stakeholders.**

Software can be useful in creating a business plan. It might come in handy for the financial projections, but for the description of the project, the market research, and the marketing strategy, more serious work is required.

The role of the business plan is crucial. It is the tool that allows you to present your project clearly. It is the ultrasound of your baby, so to speak. It allows you to see if your project is viable and if it has all the requisite attributes in place.

The business plan helps you to begin to look for and talk to investors, partners, or banks. It also helps you to convince these entities that you have a solid investment opportunity.

The business plan is also your window. Try it out on your friends, partners, or potential partners. Take their temperature and see if they will follow you. As I mentioned earlier, the business plan could be either a booster or a braking mechanism.

To those who say that this last point is useless, especially for start-ups, I reply that everyone is not equal to the task demanded by the business.

It is better be a good-looking man or woman than the opposite if you wish to find a job, for example. The same things goes for the business plan. Nowadays you look better using NTIC software, but this does not mean that your business is not worthwhile if you do not use it.

A business plan is necessary for most projects. Therefore you need to ensure that it presents clear ideas for you to discuss with investors or potential partners.

Some people no longer feel the need to have a formal business plan. This may be related to their particular activity or experience. They know their business plan by heart and whip one up in two seconds based on precedent. However, most entrepreneurs require a business plan.

Business Plan Outline

As we said earlier, the business plan is a **communication tool** that will allow you to sell your project. Its goal is to be **convincing**. Following are the components of a professional-quality business plan:

1. Executive summary

This first part should not take up more than one page. Ideally it should provide a general overview at a glance.

The executive summary should include the following:

- the matter or problem that your product or service will address or solve
- your solution
- your assets versus those of the competition
- your business model
- your team
- the expected results/income/turnover
- what you need (financing, partners, cofounder, etc.)

2. Product or service

The business plan is all about clearly describing your project, your idea. Use the exercises presented in **chapter 2**.

2.1. Description

- Describe the product or service.
- Describe the solution you bring.
- Describe the opportunities.
- Know that you are the showcase for your project.
- Introduce yourself and the other project leaders/owners.

- Let potential investors know why they should trust you. Mention the following things:
  - your profile
  - your title
  - your tasks and responsibilities

2.2. Competitive comparison

Use the exercises you completed in **chapter 2**.

2.3. Technology

Use this part, if applicable, to demonstrate the use of the technological tools that you are choosing to deploy.

3. Market analysis

Use the exercises and the research you complete in **chapter 3** to quickly present the information detailed below.

Summarize this information and present it following the outline:

3.1. Market review

3.2. Market needs

3.3. Market trends

4. Strategy and implementation

Use the exercises and the research you completed in **chapter 4** to quickly present the information detailed below:

4.1. Strategy and value proposition

Present your business model. To do this, you could use the business model mentioned in **chapter 4**, which will allow you to make your presentation simple and effective, but I would suggest using it to summarize the actual strategy that you've settled on.

4.2. Marketing strategy

This will be based on the market trends and needs (mentioned in point 3 of "Market analysis," above) and the exercises that you completed in **chapter 4**.

5. Management summary

Use the research you have done to complete the exercises in **chapter 5** to quickly present the information found below.

6. Financial plan

Use the table in **chapter 6**.

If the table you have is more complete than the one presented in the model, feel free to use the one you find to be the most relevant based on your needs and on your project.

CHAPTER 8

START YOUR BUSINESS

Now comes the time to start your business.

Normally, depending on the strength of his or her enthusiasm, it is likely at this stage that the entrepreneur has already advanced in establishing his or her network of providers, hammering out the logistics, or finding the right location for the business.

Far from being a problem, starting the business is the easy part, much easier than dealing with not having any background in start-ups, having to wait and see, gathering all the necessary elements together, meeting with the appropriate authorities, suppliers, and so forth, and signing contracts for products that you will launch to complete your project.

Thus, the start-up, although representing the end of the project development cycle and preparation, constitutes the starting point of the adventure, the birth of your baby.

Much effort has been made so far. Many other steps remain.

Why Do People Become Entrepreneurs?

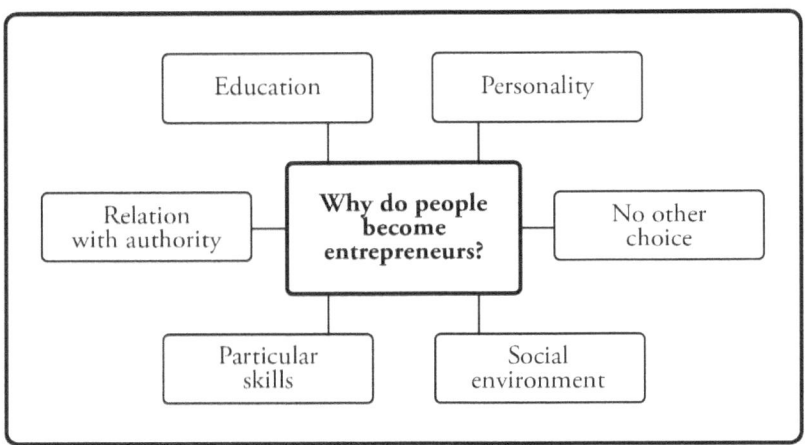

Why people become entrepreneurs

People become entrepreneurs for many reasons, one of which is that they have a degree that is too advanced, making them problematic to hire, or perhaps it is the opposite reason—too little education—with the same consequences.

The person's personality could also play an important role as some entrepreneurs cannot stand having a boss, being too ambitious and/or impatient, for example.

Perhaps the person has faced too many difficulties in his or her social environment, making it a heavy proposition to trust or hire him or her given his or her profile or background.

Some other entrepreneurs have some particular skills that either are no longer used or have yet to be used and explored. Such could be the case with artisans or creators of new technologies.

People also become entrepreneurs because they feel that they have no other choice. Perhaps they have a personal or familial situation that compels them to strike out on their own, or perhaps no job fits their needs.

Uncertainty in Entrepreneurship

> A person often meets his destiny on the road he took to avoid it.
>
> Jean de La Fontaine, French poet, 1621–1695

Uncertainty is a part of the entrepreneurial process. To manage this period of uncertainty, you must have the humility to face your own vulnerability and overcome your doubts.

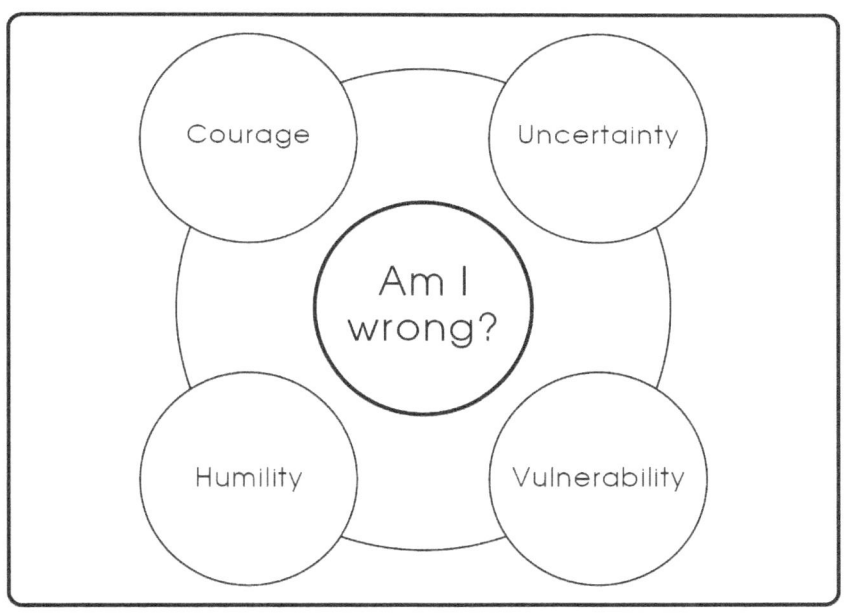

"Am I wrong?"

As an entrepreneur, one of the questions you face early in the process of starting a business is "Am I wrong?" That is, "Am I wrong in chasing my dream, which may potentially lead me to nowhere?"

As entrepreneurs, we tend to see the empty space where we want to go, ignoring the idea of whether our idea will work or not. Sometimes we are afraid that our friends and relatives will laugh at our "brilliant" idea. We may feel that we are putting ourselves in an unnecessarily complicated situation.

But the real question is, what if we are right to be doing what we're doing? What if we're right in chasing a dream that will possibly lead us somewhere?

I was surprised by a book written by a psychologist telling the life stories of people who have succeeded where they were supposed to fail.[20]

Obviously from the title of the book I felt that the subject was going to excite me. The deeper I got into the book, the happier I was to be reading it. This evidence came at a time when I had come to understand the difference between not making sense of my life, having a career, and having a vocation or a "call."

The search for money and recognition should not weigh more heavily than the search for happiness or blossoming, because it is the latter that makes you rich. These external elements, which at first seem to be the most important, become less important when your drive and your attention are elsewhere.

The irony of the story is that the money and the recognition remain merely an effect of the cause.

If we linger on this point for just a moment, we will realize that if everybody were doing something that made them feel good, all of us would probably experience fewer frustrations, and the world would be a better place.[21]

The other important part to consider is that uncertainty is part of life. Nothing is stable. We do not know when the last day of our life will arrive,

---

[20] Rom Brafman, *Succeeding When You're Supposed to Fail: The 6 Enduring Principles of High Achievement* (New York: Three Rivers, 2013).
[21] Mark Leruste, "What They Don't Tell You about Entrepreneurship," TED talk, July 19, 2017, https://www.youtube.com/watch?v=f6nxcfbDfZo&app=desktop.

how our marriage will end up, how our kids will turn out, and so forth. We do not come to earth with a guide to follow showing us how each day will work and who we will become.

Our acceptance of this situation leads to a beautiful way of seeing life. It also opens our minds to a lot of possibilities.

If you accept the fact that you do not know, then you can choose to try things and to act like anything is possible. It is sometimes necessary to admit that you do not know something. You need to accept this fact if you are to set out to discover that which you do not know. Instead of thinking, *"What will happen if I fail?",* wonder why you shouldn't try since it is possible that you may succeed.

The fear of failure will make you fail. Changing the angle, daring to try, daring to believe, and daring to show who you are will, without a doubt, take your perception to another level.

This is actually how people become inspiring. They propose new views and inspire others with their courage or vision. Think about the way that you felt when you did something that you thought you could not do. When you review your doubts, you should know that the most important thing is, more than inspiring others, to discover yourself by pushing your limits. This quality is one that is necessary for entrepreneurship; it is in the job description: *Dare to push your limits.*

> If you love what you do, you'll never have to work a day in your life.
>
> Confucius

Entrepreneur Portrait

Arnaud

The restaurant is a homey and yet modern wine bar and bistro designed for anyone looking for an extensive list of wines by the glass, affordable food to eat, and a place to meet friends in a place with a casual atmosphere and friendly service.

Arnaud is a thirty-two-year-old epicurean who was born in the Loire Valley of France. He has about ten years' experience in bars and restaurants, hotel management, and fine dining throughout Europe and Asia. A real food and wine lover, he is passionate about hospitality and culinary trends. He has been an entrepreneur for a year now, putting all his energy, his know-how, and his soul into a very exciting first restaurant project.

The following is an interview that we did with him:

How did you get the idea for opening this business?
The idea of becoming an entrepreneur had been growing within me for a very long time. The idea became bigger and bigger after the years I spent working hard for a countless number of hours for owners or employers, when I realized that I could just spend the same amount of time but be my own employer. The restaurant project grew out of a lot of frustration, going out for lunch or dinner in Hanoi and finding a poor offering of wines by the glass in most restaurants here in town. Bad value, low quality, and poor choice of wines by the glass. Do you want to get a decent glass of wine in Hanoi? Go to a five-star hotel and pay an unreasonable price for it, or just buy a bottle in a restaurant. But for the most part, people don't want to drink a whole bottle of wine on their own every day.

What is the best word or mantra to describe your mindset?
"Stop waiting for things to happen! Go out and make them happen!"

What is the message you're trying to spread?

We all have dreams! Those dreams can be either dreamed or lived. It is just a matter of choice. There is no written destiny. We all have the power to make choices and take actions that will determine our lives. The door does not open? Build your own f … g door!

What do you wish to provide to people?
For people working with me? A good working environment where each team member can be valued according to their merit and motivation, where they can learn and grow. For my customers? I want to make them feel good, feel at home, and feel well treated with top-quality, good-value food and wine and friendly service.

How long have you been involved in this activity?
Almost ten years.

Currently, how many workers are working here?
Ten.

What advice would you give to young entrepreneurs?
If you have a dream, an idea, or a project, take a bit of your free time to develop it. Investigate, take notes, and make a basic business plan. Then share your project with neutral people who have a "go for it" attitude. Do not listen to people who have a "can't be done" attitude.

CONCLUSION

When I meet people who are inspired, they inspire me to help them go in the direction that they want to take their lives. I gain satisfaction in the realization of their project, the reason for their struggles. I am convinced that the success of my business is based on their success. My business feeds me, inspires me, and motivates me to continue to grow it.

When considering the amount of time, we spend at work, we quickly realize the importance of having a happy work life. A person who is not happy and satisfied with his or her work will not make those around him or her, whether colleagues or customers, happy.

Though I may not know what makes people happy, I can give them the tools to thrive at what they do most of the time, which benefits them, their employers, and their employees and, indirectly, their families.

I choose to help entrepreneurs because the creation and evolution of their companies allows me to understand who they are. It also helps me to see that everyone and anyone has the ability to become an entrepreneur. An idea, a passion, a desire, or simply a hobby could turn out to be the new viral technology like Facebook, Uber, or Google.

> **An idea, a passion, a desire, or simply a hobby can, in time, become a new viral technology.**

Societies change, paradigms change, and capitalism changes too. I am convinced that the new economy is global, the result of an unprecedented level of sharing and collaboration.

We are no longer a race of people seeking to amass money alone; we are now looking to give meaning to life. A kind of balance is being established between the need for money to live and the need to have fun and grow.

These views may seem idealistic or completely unrealistic for some, but the balance between private life and professional life, the search for purpose and meaning, and lifelong learning all contribute to personal growth.

BIBLIOGRAPHY

BNP Paribas, "Global Entrepreneur Report 2016: 3 HC Coaching."

Brenée Brown. *The power of vulnerability: Teaching of Authenticity, Connections and courage* published April 2013

Rom Brafman. *Succeeding When You're Supposed to Fail: The 6 Enduring Principles of High Achievement.* (New York: Three Rivers, 2013).

Jeffery G. Harber. "Generations in the Workplace: Similarities and Differences." PhD dissertation, East Tennessee State University, 2011.

Eleazar Hernández. *Leading Creative Teams: Management Career Paths for Designers, Developers, and Copywriters.* (New York: Apress, 2016).

Wendy Kerr. *My New Business: A Busy Woman's Guide to Start-Up Success.* (Upper Saddle River, NJ: FT Press, 2014).

Michael Lewis. *The New New Thing: A Silicon Valley Story.* (New York: W. W. Norton, 1999).

Joan Magretta. "Why Business Models Matter." *Harvard Business Review* (May 2012).

Cynthia Montgomery. *The Strategist: Be the Leader Your Business Needs.* (New York: Harper Business, 2012).

Peter Northouse. *Leadership: Theory and Practice.* (India: Sage, 2009).

Alexander Osterwalder and Yves Pigneur. *Business Model Generation: A Handbook for Visionaries, Game Changers, and Challengers.* (New York: John Wiley and Sons, 2010).

ONLINE SOURCES

8s2Business: http://8s2business.com/

Marion Bain, "77% des auto-entreprises meurent avant cinq ans," L'Express, September 19, 2017, https://lentreprise.lexpress.fr/creation-entreprise/auto-entrepreneur/77-des-auto-entrepreneurs-periclitent-avant-cinq-ans_1944901.html.

Rebecca Burn Callander. "It's Official: Most People Are Miserable at Work." The *Telegraph*, September 18, 2015. http://www.telegraph.co.uk/finance/jobs/11871751/Its-official-most-people-are-miserable-at-work.html.

Brett Cenkus. "Millennials Will Work Hard, Just Not for Your Crappy Job." The Start-Up, November 16, 2017. https://medium.com/swlh/millennials-will-work-hard-just-not-for-your-crappy-job-82c12a1853ed.

James Chen. "Investment." Investopedia, last modified February 27, 2020. https://www.investopedia.com/terms/i/investment.asp.

Peter Fleming. "The Trials of a 2016 Job: Why So Many of Us Are Unhappy at Work." *The Guardian*, May 9, 2016. https://www.theguardian.com/commentisfree/2016/may/09/trails-of-2016-job-low-satisfaction-company-short-termism.

Richard Harroch. "20 Things All Entrepreneurs Should Know about Angel Investors." *Forbes*, February 5, 2015. https://www.forbes.com/sites/

allbusiness/2015/02/05/20-things-all-entrepreneurs-should-know-about-angel-investors/3/#2e24415f1acb.

Ryan Jenkins. "This Is Why Millennials Care So Much about Work-Life Balance." *Inc.* magazine. https://www.inc.com/ryan-jenkins/this-is-what-millennials-value-most-in-a-job-why.html.

Mark Leruste. "What They Don't Tell You about Entrepreneurship." TED talk. https://www.youtube.com/watch?v=f6nxcfbDfZo&app=desktop.

"Les chiffres clés des entreprises en France en 2019." Wydden, September 10, 2019. https://wydden.com/chiffres-cles-entreprises-en-france/.

Dani Mansfield. "15 Creative Exercises that Are Better than Brainstorming." *Marketing*, last modified September 30, 2018. https://blog.hubspot.com/marketing/creative-exercises-better-than-brainstorming.

Randi Sherman. "The Difference between Value Propositions, Taglines, and Slogans." The Social Calling, July 21, 2019. https://www.thesocialcalling.com/the-difference-between-value-propositions-taglines-and-slogans/.

"Survie des entreprises à 5 ans." Petite-Enterprise, November 19, 2012. https://www.petite-entreprise.net/P-137-87-G1-survie-des-entreprises-a-5-ans.html.

Wikipedia, s.v. "Uber," last modified May 20, 2020. https://en.wikipedia.org/wiki/Uber.

www.ingramcontent.com/pod-product-compliance
Lightning Source LLC
Chambersburg PA
CBHW021416210526
45463CB00001B/393